UNFORGETTABLE RANGERS

GAMES & MOMENTS FROM THE PRESS BOX

BY: MATTHEW BLITTNER

ISBN: 978-0-578-44326-3
ISBN-13: 978-0-578-44326-3

DEDICATION

In this world, it's not enough to merely believe in yourself. Rather, you need others to believe in you as well.

To that end, this book would not have been completed without the support of my family and friends.

Specifically, I'd like to dedicate this book to my parents -- Mandi and Seth -- and sister Tara for their constant support even during the toughest times.

And to my friends -- Arianna Rappy, Stef Hicks, Leanna Gryak, Maggie Wince, Walt Bonne, Daniel Greene, Jared Fertig, Peter Koutros, Jason Russo and Robert DeVita -- who were always there for me when I needed them and I thank them for that.

CONTENTS

INTRODUCTION

As an Original Six franchise, the New York Rangers are one of the most storied teams in NHL history.

And in their over 90 years of existence, the Rangers -- as well as their fans, writers and broadcasters -- have bore witness to numerous unforgettable games and moments.

For starters, who could ever forget The "Silver Fox," Lester Patrick putting himself in net as the Blueshirts' emergency netminder during the middle of the 1927-28 Stanley Cup Final against the Montreal Canadiens.

From the team's inception at the beginning of the 1926-27 season, through the 1939-40 Stanley Cup Final, the Blueshirts captured three Stanley Cup championships. And during that time period, Rangers supporters were privileged to watch "The Bread Line" (Bill Cook, Frank Boucher and Bun Cook) at the peak of its' powers.

Fast-forward to 1950, it had been a decade since the Seventh Avenue Skaters last won it all.

But the 1949-50 campaign wasn't kind to New York. An underwhelming Rangers squad barely managed to eke into the playoffs as the fourth and final seed.

However, the playoffs were a chance to rewrite their story.

Led by Bench Boss, Lynn Patrick, the Blueshirts caught fire and made it to the Stanley Cup Final where they faced the Detroit Red Wings.

A back-and-forth series saw slender Rangers' center, Don "Bones" Raleigh etch his name in the history books as he recorded the game-winning goal in overtime, not once, but twice in Games 4 and 5. Raleigh's heroics had the New York sextet one win from The Cup, but Detroit had other ideas and forced Game 7.

Sadly, Detroit wound up winning the game and the series in double-overtime after Blueshirts' forward, Dunc Fisher just missed winning the game in the first-overtime period when he clanged one off the post.

From there, the Rangers took a hiatus from the Stanley Cup Final; not making another appearance in the Championship Round until the 1971-72 season.

The late-1960's and early-1970's proved a most memorable time for RangersTown as the team was led by the incomparable "GAG Line" -- as in Goal A Game Line -- consisting of Rod Gilbert, Jean Ratelle and Vic Hadfield.

With The GAG Line leading the way, it seemed inevitable the Rangers would break their Stanley Cup drought. However, while they led the team to the 1971-72 Final against the Boston Bruins, they fell in six games; partially because a broken bone in Ratelle's foot sidelined him near the end of the regular season and prevented him from suiting up in the playoffs.

The GAG Line was broken up in 1974 when Hadfield was traded to Pittsburgh. And a year later, Ratelle followed him out the door as he was traded to Boston as part of a package for Phil Esposito.

Meanwhile, the New Yorkers made it back to The Cup Final in 1979, but were outmatched by the Montreal Canadiens; losing the series in five games.

From there, the team went through a middling stretch where it was good enough to make the playoffs most years, but not good enough to win it all. That is, until it returned to prominence in the early-1990's.

Led by Edmonton Oilers imports -- namely Mark Messier -- the Rangers were a team to be reckoned with, but "The Curse," still managed to survive a few more years.

Then came the magical 1993-94 campaign.

From the start of Training Camp things felt different around the team. And by mid-season it was apparent something special was in the air; or rather, on the ice.

Not to get caught up in the hype surrounding his team, Head Coach Mike Keenan insisted G.M. Neil Smith bolster the team's roster in order to improve its' chances at finally winning the Stanley Cup.

An unforgettable power struggle took place, and in the end, Keenan won out, as Smith brought in reinforcements.

When the playoffs opened, the President's Trophy-winning Rangers were considered heavy favorites to win The Cup. And quick dispatches of the Islanders and Capitals further fueled that notion.

But the New Jersey Devils were waiting in the Eastern Conference Final and they had no plans on being swept aside in the Rangers quest to end their 54-year Cup drought.

An unforgettable series -- which has spawned several books dedicated strictly to regaling those memorable games -- ensued.

From Messier's bold, "We Will Win Game Six," to Howie Rose's jubilant, "MATTEAU! MATTEAU! MATTEAU!" the seven-game series between New York and New Jersey will live on forever in the hearts and minds of the Blueshirts Faithful.

And don't forget, according to Rose, the Rangers had, "one more hill to climb baby, but it's Mt. Vancouver!"

The thrilling and sometimes heart-attack inducing seven-game triumph over the Canucks gave the Rangers their first Stanley Cup championship since 1940, and along the way, created a set of memories that, "Will Last A Lifetime!"

From there, the Blueshirts endured some lean years, although they did have the honor of having The Great One, Wayne Gretzky play for them for the final three-years of his illustrious career.

Eventually, someone new was required to take over as the face of the franchise.

Enter Henrik Lundqvist.

Arguably the most decorated goalie in Rangers' history, Lundqvist has manned the pipes since the 2005-06 season and in that time he's proceeded to rewrite not just the Blueshirts' record books, but the NHL's as well. And while, he has yet to taste the sweet nectar of a championship, Lundqvist has more than lived up to his nickname of, "King Henrik."

Among "The King's" many memorable accomplishments is a four-season stretch from 2012-2015 when he led the Rangers to three Eastern Conference Finals and one Stanley Cup appearance (2014).

With these and so many other unforgettable moments littered across Rangers history, it is the duty of those covering the team from the press box -- or the TV/Radio booths -- to keep these memories and moments alive.

The eyes of Sam Rosen, Dave Maloney, John Giannone, Joe Micheletti, Kenny Albert, Howie Rose, Rick Carpiniello, Allan Kreda, Pat O'Keefe, Don La Greca, John Davidson, Stan Fischler and others, have witnessed over a century of combined Blueshirts' seasons. It is through their recollections that I bring the stories of some of the most unforgettable games and moments in Rangers history to the forefront of RangersTown.

In fact, some games are so unforgettable that more than one person chose to share their story from that game. But what makes these overlapping games and moments special is that each person has their own recollection based upon their differing vantage points.

For example, Rosen, Giannone and Rose all talked about Game 7 of the 1994 Eastern Conference Final against the Devils. But each person had a different role and therefore a different focus. Sam was on television, Howie radio and John was a writer. So all three had various aspects of the game that they each chose to focus on and that's what makes each of their stories unique.

1 KENNY ALBERT (NHL RADIO)
GAME 7: 1994 STANLEY CUP FINAL (@MSG)
JUNE 14, 1994
NYR 3, VAN 2

BACKGROUND

If you're a fan of professional sports, chances are you've heard of The Albert Family.

Kenny Albert, along with his father Marv Albert, and uncles Steve Albert and Al Albert makeup arguably the most famous -- and successful -- broadcaster family in America.

Regardless of what sport you fancy, you've likely listened to at least one of the Albert men calling a game at some point. After all, the oldest, Marv, began his broadcasting career in 1963.

Now, let's get back to Kenny.

Growing up with a famous father and two famous uncles, Kenny Albert was born to be a broadcaster. In fact, at the age of five he was given a tape recorder for his birthday and he immediately started recording himself calling games. And he hasn't stopped.

Kenny practically grew up at Madison Square Garden and as a teenager in high school; he was fortunate enough to be in the right place at the right time.

"When I was a sophomore in high school on Long Island, I was very fortunate," recalled Albert. "Cox Cable came to my school in Port Washington to film a girl's basketball game and I met the producer and volunteered to do the play-by-play. Over the next three years in high school, I did hundreds of games for them; hockey, basketball, football, baseball, soccer, whatever I could get my hands on."

From there, his broadcasting career took him to NYU.

"I went to NYU and they had a radio station; WNYU," Albert told me. "We had a basketball team, but no football or baseball. We also had a club hockey team, which I actually played on. But I did the basketball broadcasts. From there I had some internships and other jobs during college. Meanwhile, I ended up filling-in on some Islanders pre- and post-game shows and even on some broadcasts during my senior year.

"My first NHL game was actually the Islanders at Winnipeg, on December 2, 1989, while I was still in college. That was the first NHL Game I did and I wound up using that tape as a demo reel. I sent that tape around and got a job with the Baltimore Skipjacks of the American Hockey League in the summer of 1990 to do their radio broadcasts as well as PR, marketing, ticket sales and anything else. At that level everybody did everything in the office.

"I was there for two years and then wound up getting hired by Home Team Sports in Washington to do the Capitals home games on television; starting in 1992. I did three years there and then joined the Rangers on the radio side in 1995. I also did Fox Hockey back in the late-nineties and now NBC Hockey for the last eight or nine years."

MOST UNFORGETTABLE RANGERS GAME

Like most native New Yorkers, Kenny Albert was -- and still is -- a sports man through and through. And when it came to hockey, there was only one team he could call his favorite.

That's right, you guessed, it; Kenny Albert's favorite team was...The Vancouver Canucks. (Go ahead; take a minute to digest that. Don't worry; his reasoning is actually pretty sound). Thanks to his father's influence, Kenny lived and breathed sports broadcasting his entire life. And, in addition to the men in his family, Kenny Albert also idolized Vancouver Canucks' play-by-play man, Jim Robson.

But fear not, for Kenny's second favorite team was the New York Rangers.

So imagine what a young Kenny Albert must have been going through when he found out that his next assignment would be to call the Rangers vs. Canucks Stanley Cup Final for NHL Radio.

"As broadcasters, we don't root on the air," explained Albert. "But personally, going into that series, even though I had been a Canucks fan as a youngster, I wanted to see the Rangers win The Cup; especially here at MSG after 54 years."

KENNY ALBERT: "So the story behind this is that in 1993, Howie Rose and Mike Keenan were doing the Stanley Cup Final between L.A.

and Montreal for NHL Radio. Then, in 1994, Keenan was hired to coach the Rangers. Meanwhile, Rose was still doing NHL Radio, but he also had his Rangers radio gig.

"During the Conference Final against the Devils -- the famous series against the Devils -- I was working in DC where the Capitals had been eliminated in the second-round by the Rangers. And I got a phone call one day asking me if I would be interested in doing The Finals for NHL Radio if the Rangers made it because of Howie's Rangers' responsibilities. So now I was rooting for the Rangers hard at that point. It's ironic because they had been one of my favorite teams as a youngster -- the other being the Canucks -- and now they were on a crash course.

"There I am, watching Game Seven, Rangers vs. Devils, from my apartment in Maryland and hoping the Rangers are going to win. Because, remember, if the Devils win, I don't get to work The Final. And at 26-years-old it would be a huge opportunity. Anyway, the Rangers went on to win and I got to work The Final."

So, now you have a 26-year-old Kenny Albert getting ready to live out his boyhood dream. And in the midst of living that dream, he took part in one of the most heart-wrenching, unforgettable and emotional games in Rangers history; Game Seven of the 1994 Stanley Cup Final.

Remember, it had been 54 long, torturous years for the Blueshirts and their fans.

A seeming curse set by former-New York Americans coach-turned-owner, Red Dutton was supposedly at the root of the Rangers' problems. During World War Two, many players went off to fight in the war and that left the NHL in a tough spot. Among the teams hit hardest were the New York Americans. So, Dutton decided to temporarily fold the franchise until after the war. And after doing so, Dutton reluctantly agreed to serve as League President at the behest of the other owners, but only if they promised he would get his team back at the end of the war.

However, when the war ended, the other owners supposedly reneged on the deal; leaving Dutton furious. In the heat of the moment, Dutton blamed the Rangers for this betrayal and evidently cursed the team to, "never win another Stanley Cup in his lifetime." From that moment, until Dutton's passing in 1987, the Blueshirts were Cup-less.

So, when The Messiah, Mark Messier, arrived in New York in 1991, fans were hopeful that "Dutton's Curse" would finally be laid to rest. Unfortunately, it took a few more years -- until the 1993-94 season -- for the curse to be broken.

Finally, after 54-years of waiting, Rangers fans could wait no longer; it was now or never. The pieces were in place, but could the 1993-94 New York Rangers do what their predecessors had failed to do for over half a century? Could they be the ones to end 'The Curse' and capture the most sought after trophy in all of sports -- The Stanley Cup?

Here's Kenny Albert with the call:

KENNY ALBERT: "It was Game Seven and everybody was nervous. Not just Rangers fans, but the whole city. If you think back to how New York was during the Yankees' World Series runs each October; that's how it was for the Rangers, but it was June. It was all over the back page; everyday people were so excited. And remember, the Knicks were in the NBA Finals at the time as well; so, both teams were simultaneously in The Finals and the city was going crazy.

"I remember, meeting people for lunch around Bryant Park earlier that day and just thinking how hot it was. And I remember taking a cab down to The Garden; probably got there a few hours before the game. But first, let me take you back a couple nights to Game Five.

"The Rangers had a three-one lead in the series and when you woke up the morning of June ninth -- the day of Game Five -- on the back page of every tabloid in New York was the Stanley Cup. I don't remember the exact headlines, but they were something to the effect of 'The Cup Is Ours' and 'The Cup Will Be In The Building Tonight;' stuff like that.

"Everybody thought the Rangers were going to win it that night. Tickets were going for astronomical prices, and then the Rangers fell behind in the game; 3-0. But, then the Rangers came back to tie it in the third period and the place was going crazy! I was in the upper press box (this was before The Garden was renovated in 2013) when they tied it in the third period. It was just a crazy third period. And I'm roughly 50-feet from where we are right now; calling the game with Sherry Ross, who was my analyst for the series.

"The building was going crazy, and then roughly 30 seconds after the Rangers tied it, Dave Babych scored to take back the lead for Vancouver. From there the Canucks went on to score twice more; winning the game 6-3.

"As a little sidebar for you, I met my wife Barbara that night after the game. You see, if the Rangers win that game then I probably go to some kind of celebration party and probably never meet the person that turns out to be my wife. What happened was, a good friend of mine named Jerry Coleman, who was a radio guy in Baltimore back then, was in town doing some voiceover work. We had met back in 1990 and became good friends; even doing a radio show together in Baltimore at one point. He went to Ithaca College in New York and had three good friends who were all roommates; my wife being one of them and her two roommates.

"So, Jerry happened to be up in New York doing some voiceover work that week and he had dinner with my wife and one of her roommates. The three of them went to dinner and he told me to call him after the game to see if maybe we'll meet up. I said to him, 'if the Rangers win, probably not because I'll go to some kind of a celebration.' And remember this was before cell phones.

"But they did have payphones in the auxiliary press room, which was on the 31st street side of The Garden -- where they used to keep the animals during the circus. So, when the Rangers lost, I ended up calling Jerry, who was at my future wife's apartment. And that ended up being the first time I met my wife. And then I flew to Vancouver the next day for Game Six before coming back to New York for Game Seven.

"Back then, Kevin McDonald (now a scout for the St. Louis Blues) was the Assistant PR guy for the Rangers. And back then; they actually let the media buy tickets to The Final before the series started. Kevin was in charge of that. In fact, they had a whole section of tickets for the media to buy; so I bought six for that whole series that I gave to friends. They sat behind the net on the Eighth Avenue side of The Garden. I believe some of my friends still have their ticket stubs from the series. They were in the 200-level; probably face value of like $40, which in The Final is an unbelievable deal. So I had six friends at every game thanks to Kevin. And there was just so much anticipation and nervousness in the air.

"The Rangers had a three-one series lead and were forced to play Game Seven. They had not won The Cup in 54-years; just the whole atmosphere in the building, it was electric. And then I'll never forget, Brian Leetch scored that early goal on the 'empty net' to give the Rangers the 1-0 lead.

"Leetch's goal was scored on the Eighth Avenue end of the ice and shortly thereafter, Adam Graves scored to put the team up 2-0. At that time people were feeling pretty good from the Rangers' standpoint. After all, that Rangers' team was loaded, especially with all the guys who had won Cups with Edmonton, like: Graves, (Jeff) Beukeboom, Kevin Lowe, (Craig) MacTavish, Glenn Anderson, Esa Tikkanen and (Mark) Messier.

"In all, there were seven former-Edmonton Oilers on that team. And then you also had Brian Leetch, who wound up winning the Conn Smythe as Playoff MVP, and you had the brilliant goaltending of Mike Richter, who had been terrific that whole series; including stopping Pavel Bure on a penalty-shot in Game Four.

"And don't forget, Vancouver also had a pretty good team, what with having Bure, Trevor Linden, Kirk McLean, Greg Adams, who had scored the overtime goal for them here in Game One, and Geoff

Courtnall. But I think when you look at the rosters; the Rangers certainly should have had the edge, at least on paper. And that's kind of how it went over the first four games as the Rangers built a three-one series lead.

"But remember, you also had the background issue of what was going on with Mike Keenan. During the playoffs it came out that Keenan was potentially talking to Detroit about being their coach. (He eventually went to St. Louis.) And when you think back to the Devils series, the Rangers were down three to two going into Game Six. Then Messier came out with 'The Guarantee,' but they were still pretty close to getting eliminated in the Conference Finals.

"So, while they pretty much had had a cakewalk through their first-round sweep of the Islanders and their five-game victory over the Capitals in Round Two, the Rangers were on the brink.

"There was just a lot of stuff going on around the Rangers. But, Messier scored the hat-trick in Game Six, and along with the brilliant goaltending of Richter, they were able to force a Game Seven and eventually go on to The Final.

"So, with all of that in their rearview mirror, I think people were feeling pretty good about the Rangers being up 2-0 in Game Seven against the Canucks. And then, shortly after Trevor Linden brought Vancouver within 2-1 early in the second period, Messier scored on the power-play to put the Rangers up 3-1. But Linden wasn't done as he scored again, this time, early in the third period, to make it a one-goal game with something like 15 minutes to go in the game.

"Now the tension inside the building was at any all-time high. To borrow a phrase from Dave Maloney, 'it became a tension convention.' Essentially, now anything could happen. In fact, Nathan Lafayette hit the post behind Richter at one point and somehow the puck just stayed out; but it was that close to being three-three.

"And what I really remember is Richter making some huge saves to keep the Rangers' lead intact. There were chances at both ends, but the Rangers were kind of just hanging on; all the way down to the final minute. At one point, I looked around the stands and there was just so much white because everybody was either waving a towel or wearing the Rangers white jerseys, which the team used to wear at home. And then came a couple of icings; the last of which stopped the clock with 1.1 seconds to go.

"As time wound down, everybody was on their feet and it was hot in The Garden; I was sweating. And I remember, I had a camera -- we didn't have cell phones then so these weren't camera phones -- a real camera with me. So, as the, game's ending and the celebration is starting

-- while I'm still on the air -- I was actually taking pictures of what was going on on the ice. And I still have those photos at home.

"Meanwhile, that final icing kind of put a halt to everything.

"It was debatable if that final icing should have been called, and then the refs went and added an extra half-second to the clock. It probably could have gone either way and not many people in the building were happy with the call, but everybody kind of reset and got ready for the final face-off.

"With 1.6 seconds remaining, even though a goal could be scored, I felt it was pretty unlikely. Plus, the Rangers had one of the best face-off men in the league in Craig MacTavish. But until the clock hits zero you never know.

"But then you had the final face-off and it was just bedlam. And of course, Sam (Rosen) said it best: 'This one will last a lifetime!' The 54-years of frustration were finally over and there was that fan, holding the now famous sign that read, 'Now I Can Die In Peace.' Overall, it was a magical night and it's hard to believe it was almost 25-years ago.

"And on the radio, I had my call of, 'Say Good-Bye To The Ghost Of 1940!'

"Again, it's almost 25-years later, but in some ways it seems like it was yesterday. And in other ways it really does seem like 25-years ago."

After the game, while the players celebrated on the ice, Kenny stayed in the radio booth to provide commentary on the post-game show.

"We had a pretty long post-game," recalled Albert. "We had a sideline reporter who was down on the ice doing interviews. So I think a lot of what was going on -- on radio the listeners can't see what's going on -- we had to describe to our audience. The players were celebrating; they had all thrown off their gloves and got rid of their sticks and were piling on top of Mike Richter.

"Then the Conn Smythe Trophy was awarded to Brian Leetch, so we threw down to the PA announcer for that and then we went back and forth describing who was skating around with The Cup. Overall, I believe we were on the air for something like 30 minutes after the game ended. I couldn't even make my way to the locker room; it was just too crowded.

"Then, as I was heading out through where the theatre lobby currently is, I saw Mike Keenan and Mark Messier running through the area; holding The Cup up in the air. For me, it was a great moment to see. And if I had to pick one snapshot from that night, it would be the moment when Gary Bettman handed Messier The Cup. You could just see the look of joy on his face when he held it up; and remember, he had already won it five times with Edmonton. But he was the savior here in New York."

COMMENTARY FROM OTHERS AT THE GAME

AL TRAUTWIG: "I remember being reminded of how 18,000 people can be as quiet as they were; they were scared to death. They were nervous. The building was not loud and crazy. In the end it was, but not during the game. It was very tense and I think it was because of what had gone on in the series prior to that.

"Game 5 was, 'they were going to win.' It was the front page of The Post, the front page of The Daily News and all of a sudden it's Vancouver leading 3-1. And then, all of a sudden, the Rangers tie the game.

"I ran up to my wife and son and before I could even get to them, Vancouver scored to take the lead and win the game. Then we went to Vancouver for Game 6 and there was a riot after the game with people pounding the bus. Other than death, it was the saddest I've ever been in my life.

"So, Game 7 was, 'okay, it's the last chance.' The building was really quiet. It was a close game; a one-goal game. I'm between the benches and Mike Keenan is chewing on ice and Nathan LaFayette hits the post. It was shocking just how perilous the whole thing was. And then, Kevin Collins, the linesman, I think it was 1.1 seconds to go and the Rangers iced the puck. He thought it was necessary to add half a second to the clock; so 1.6 I'm pretty sure.

"I don't think I've ever been more nervous for 1.6 seconds in my entire life. Looking back now that it's been so many years, I'm not sure there's ever going to be a Game 7 anymore with a bunch of old guys playing in a game like that. The game has just gotten so young. But there's Craig MacTavish taking the most important face-off in Rangers history, and other than marriage and birth, it was the greatest night of my life.

"I remember being in the locker room, it was about 100 degrees, and Adam Graves poured ice-cold champagne down my back. It was one of the greatest sensations I've ever had. We were on the air until one o'clock in the morning I believe. We just kept going and going and going. And I think it was because we all knew or felt that that was going to be one of the greatest days and it was never going to be repeated.

"When you do something like that and you recognize it, it's a really cool feeling. I wanted that night to go on forever. And I remember getting home -- there's no NHL Network, no 24-hour anything -- and I went and turned on my television and I couldn't relive the game. I just felt so helpless. I remember sitting in my office just going, 'wait a minute, why can't I watch this game again?' It was a great night."

MOST UNFORGETTABLE RANGERS MOMENT

Having lived out his boyhood dream of calling the Stanley Cup Final, Kenny Albert had climbed his personal Mt. Everest. But it isn't the only memorable Rangers' moment he's been apart of.

20-years after the Blueshirts ended the fabled curse, they had yet to return to the Promised Land.

But that all changed during the 2013-14 season.

Under the guidance of new head coach, Alain Vigneault, the New York sextet built upon an already solid foundation and returned to The Cup Final for the first time since winning it all in 1994.

And once again, Kenny Albert bore witness to the Rangers miraculous rise.

KENNY ALBERT: "That whole post-season run was truly memorable. That sixth game against Montreal in the Eastern Conference Final, when they won 1-0 to get back to the Stanley Cup Final was a terrific moment. When they won that series, that was the loudest I've heard The Garden since they won The Cup in 1994. And then there was the series against the Kings; from overtime goals to the big saves by Henrik Lundqvist. But since they wound up losing to the Kings, I would have to say it was Game Six against the Canadiens that I would pick as my most memorable.

"But, if I can go to sort of a broader picture for a minute. The time period between 2012 and 2015, there were, so many great games and overtime goals; including Derek Stepan's game-winner against Washington.

"Another biggie was Game Seven in Pittsburgh that same year, when the Rangers went down three-one in the series but Marty St. Louis -- whose Mother passed away during the series -- scored an unbelievable goal, on Mother's Day no less to bring the Rangers back to life. I'll never forget, it was one of the best goals I've ever seen. Of course, Henrik Lundqvist was at his absolute best during the final five minutes of that game. Some of the saves he made were just unbelievable. And that win sent the Rangers to the Eastern Conference Final where they played Montreal.

"Overall, that group played so many great games and had so many memorable moments between 2012 and 2015."

2 RICK CARPINIELLO (JOURNAL NEWS)
GAME 6: 1994 EASTERN CONFERENCE FINAL (@BRENDAN BYRNE ARENA)
MAY 25, 1994
NYR 4, NJD 2

BACKGROUND

When you've been around the game as long as Rick Carpiniello has, nothing really surprises you anymore. From the hottest points in the Rangers-Islanders rivalry, to the Rangers winning their first Stanley Cup in 54-years, all the way to the Present Day incarnation of the Blueshirts, Carpiniello has witnessed as many unforgettable Rangers moments as just about anyone on the planet Earth.

But how did he come to be such a keeper of New York's sensational history?

"It's a funny story," said Carpiniello. "I mean, I had dropped out of college and I was working in a mail room in Greenwich, Connecticut, and I found out that my local paper in Westchester was looking for kids to cover High School football games. It was like 10 bucks on Saturdays. So I signed up to do that and I started covering High School football games in 1976.

"Before long I got hired, one thing led to another and by 1978-79, I was doubling up on my local High School coverage with some Rangers coverage. And that's lasted quite a while. It's now called The Journal News. But back then it was the Westchester, Rockland newspapers -- there were nine of them -- but they were all pretty much the same paper."

Rick Carpiniello's tenure took him through some of the highest -- and lowest -- points in Rangers' history. But before I reveal which game he chose as his most unforgettable, here is a completed timeline of his journalist career.

"I was laid off by the Journal News in 2016, so I was out of work for awhile," explained Carpiniello. "I free-lanced for MSG Networks, which was really fun. I really enjoyed that. And believe it or not, I worked for the United States Postal Service for a couple months before I was hired by The Athletic."

Now that you've gotten to know Rick's full story, let's delve into which game he considers to be his most unforgettable.

MOST UNFORGETTABLE RANGERS GAME

The 1993-94 New York Rangers were on a mission -- and that mission was to end a 54-year long Stanley Cup drought. But this wasn't anything new for the team, the franchise, or its' fan base. In fact, the Blueshirts Faithful -- by this time -- had been well versed in the gut wrenching history of their beloved team.

From the painful ending to the 1950 Stanley Cup Final, to the "Close But No Cigar" teams of the late 1960s and early 1970s, to the surprise Cup-run in 1979, all the way to the early 1990s, Rangers supporters had suffered more than their fair share of heartbreaking moments.

So, by the time the 1993-94 season came around, New York's loyal followers had had enough. And from the start of the season, things felt different around the team. Perhaps it was their trip to London? Or maybe it had something to do with new Head Coach, Mike Keenan? Or, maybe it was just their time to finally shine? Well, one thing is for sure, these Rangers were different from their predecessors. And that sentiment led to a President's Trophy regular season, as the League's top team.

Therefore, when the playoffs began, there was enhanced optimism surrounding the 7th Avenue Skaters. And a first-round demolition of the Islanders further fueled the belief that there was something special going on with the Rangers

On to the second-round and the Rangers disposed of the Capitals in a handy five-games; setting up a date with destiny against their hated rivals, the New Jersey Devils.

The Eastern Conference Final between New York and New Jersey would pit the NHL's two top teams against each other in a thrilling, dramatic series, where the winner would not only have bragging rights, but also a chance to compete for the most sought after prize in all of sports; Lord Stanley's fabled chalice, the Stanley Cup.

A Game 1 double-overtime victory by the Devils put New York in an early hole, but the Broadway Blueshirts stormed back to win Games 2 and 3 (Game 3 in double-overtime) to take a 2-1 lead in the best-four-of-seven-series.

But the Devils righted their ship with a win in Game 4, evening the series at two games apiece. Then came the classic "swing game" in Game 5, the winner of which, would be one win away from burying their opponent and moving on to face the Canucks in the Stanley Cup Final.

In a "must-win" game for both teams, it was the Devils who came out on top, by the score of 4-1; thus putting New York on the brink of elimination.

It couldn't go down this way, thought Rangers fans everywhere. Not another too soon playoff exit. Where was all the promise this team had shown throughout the regular season and the first two rounds of the playoffs? The Rangers couldn't really lose to a team Wayne Gretzky once labeled a, "Mickey Mouse" Organization, could they?

Things looked bleak for New York, especially when they wouldn't be playing Game 6 in the friendly confines of Madison Square Garden. A trip across the Hudson isn't exactly a big deal; it's only about 14 miles by car. But in this instance, it may as well have been Earth to Pluto.

Could the Rangers save their season? Or would it go up in flames? Rick Carpiniello was there and he can tell you the whole story.

Rick, the floor is yours.

RICK CARPINIELLO: "Well obviously the big day was the day before, when there was chaos among the Rangers at the time; there were situations with their injuries. (Mike) Keenan was creating chaos. In Game 4 he did not pull Glenn Healy for an extra skater at the end of the game and the guys thought he kind of quit. It was only 3-1 and he didn't pull his goalie to try and get an extra player on. So there was a lot of chaos going on and a lot of controversy regarding who was hurt and how badly they were hurting; including (Brian) Leetch and (Mark) Messier.

"During Game 4 he had benched pretty much everyone: Leetch, (Stephane) Matteau, (Brian) Noonan and at some point Messier too. And he pulled (Mike) Richter and put Glenn Healy in goal. Leetch was not even going out for the first power-play, he was going on for the second power-play, but he was pretty much benched otherwise.

"At one point, Jay Wells, who's a veteran player, who'd never come close to winning a Stanley Cup in his life, turned and begged the coaches, 'bench me, please bench me, put Leetch back out there, we want to win.' And it didn't happen. Leetch was hurt; he did have a bad shoulder. He was having it frozen, but he was playing through it and he continued to insist it wasn't affecting his play, even though it obviously was.

"Then he benched Messier for a little bit too and so, that caused a lot of chaos. And Chaos is a term that should be Keenan's middle name, because it was just that chaotic around that time. So, they're practicing at Playland -- it's a small rink, with a small makeshift media room, because there's no real media room there -- and there's probably 100 to 150 reporters from all over North America and they're wondering what's going on with Keenan. Well, Keenan had Barry Watkins, the PR guy, summon the six beat writers and calls them into his office; just leaving the other 100 or so outside and orders us to turn off our recorders, put our notebooks down, because he's going to go off the record for the first time all year. That was his only year here and he never went off the record before or after.

"He started with the first thing, saying, 'Leetch's shoulder is fucked.' And then he went on to list some of the other injuries. (Adam) Graves had this big laceration on the back of his leg and he had a bad back and Messier was dealing with some kind of rib cage or back injury. Noonan had a knee and Matteau had his shoulder. He was going on and on and now we're thinking, 'how do we write this because it's off the record.' And we pretty much didn't, except, maybe we hinted at this is what's probably going on. When the meeting ended, we left the room and the other 100 or so writers wanted to know what we talked about, what was going on and we couldn't even tell them.

"I think most of us honored the off the record tone, but I think we also wrote that these guys were seriously hurt. And the funny part, of course, was that the game notes came out for the next game and under injuries it said the Rangers had no injuries to report; so that's always the kicker. So, Keenan addressed the rest of the guys, the rest of the media, and he said, 'we have injuries just like everybody else, but there's nothing serious.'

"I don't even know if he was ever asked about why in Game 4 he didn't pull Glenn Healy, down 3-1 late in the game for an extra attacker. It was almost as if he'd given up at that point. And this was before even the swirling rumors of him negotiating with the Detroit. I mean, you talk about chaos, that creeped in later in the Stanley Cup Final. But one other thing about Game 6 was, all of a sudden, there was a new guy behind the bench, who nobody had ever seen before, and his name was Scott Gelbs.

"So, a guy with a mustache, who nobody had ever seen before was on the Rangers' bench for Game 6 at the Meadowlands. Apparently he was some kind of a physical trainer or physical therapist or a chiropractor or something. He might've been there for Graves. But you want to talk about bizarre, showing up in Game 6 and there's a new guy on the bench.

"Also there were rumors Keenan wasn't too thrilled with their medical trainer, Dave Smith at that time, because of all the injuries. And so, he did this to show up Dave Smith. So yeah, Chaos again was his middle name.

"So they ended up losing Game 5 to go down 3-2, and then it really got crazy. So there's Messier, standing at his locker at their Rye Playland practice facility, with a big crowd around him; microphones, newspaper guys and television cameras. And he said, 'we're going to win the game.'

"He went on the whole thing about, we've done it before and we know we can win. We feel we can win and we're going to go in and win and come back for Game 7. He never said, 'guarantee.' He never said, 'we will win.' It was kind of innocuous in the tone, in that he didn't say anything outlandish. When he was done, we kind of looked at each other and we said, 'he just said we're going to win, right?' And everybody kind of nodded.

"In fact, it was so different than you would expect, it wasn't a boastful guarantee. It was so unusually put that some of the television stations didn't even use the sound bite, which was kind of crazy. But he did promise they would win, he did not guarantee it. But there was the story.

"You mentally prepare for when there's going to be a big story. You get in your mind what you're going to write if this happens and what you're going to write if that happens. In my mind, I'm writing, holy cow The Curse lives. This great team, the best team in the NHL by a lot, which did all this -- they sold their soul to the Devil to get this particular coach, who made all of these ridiculous trades during the season at the trade deadline and just put a whole new roster on the ice for the Stanley Cup playoffs.

"It's not going to work and they're going to lose again. It's going to be 54 years and counting and then what do you do? So, at that point, that's the story I'm getting ready to write, thinking they may win, they may not win. And even if they do, then they still have to win another one. So there's a pretty good chance I'm going to be writing an obituary tonight instead of a story about Mark Messier's guarantee.

"Mark said years later that he didn't realize what he had done until the next morning, driving in with Leetch and Leetch told him about the newspapers. He said he didn't realize at the time that not only would all his teammates see it, which was the point of the promise -- he was trying to fire them up and give them confidence -- but so would all of New York, New Jersey and the Devils.

"He didn't realize that and he kind of said, 'oh no.' But, at that point he also said, 'it doesn't really matter. What I was trying to do was give my teammates confidence and I hope that's what I did.' Now we get to the game and he didn't give his teammates confidence. It really almost backfired on him and almost blew up in his face because the first half of the game, they were awful and he was awful too.

"They had nothing going except Mike Richter. They were down 2-0, and Richter was keeping it from going 3-0, 4-0 and 5-0. He was the only thing keeping it from that. And I think the point in the game I most remember, was Mike Keenan calling time out. I believe it was early second period, but it might've been late first. I think it was early second and he didn't say a word. He just looked around the bench and didn't say anything to anybody. So the guys were looking around at the Assistant Coaches, Dick Todd and Colin Campbell and they were kind of not sure what to do.

"Then they started looking at Messier and Messier looked like he didn't know what to say. So it was kind of a really awkward time out that not much was accomplished. And in fact, after the timeout, the Rangers were worse for quite a while.

"It just got to the point where you're like, 'oh my God, this is going to be it. This is going to be 54 years in a row without a Stanley Cup; just because of the chaos going on around this team the last three games.' But then something clicked and a lot of people point to the moment Mike Keenan put Alex Kovalev on Messier's line instead of Glenn Anderson. So, it was (Adam) Graves, Messier and Kovalev. And that may have been (the turning point), although, I still think the two best players in the game that weren't named Messier were Richter and Leetch.

"Kovalev got a goal from Messier to put them in the game. The thing was, they finally did something that resembled the way they'd played pretty much all year and that was aggressive, attacking, using their speed. The hockey player saying, which probably goes back to God knows when is, you're one shot away and once you make it a one-goal game, you're one shot away. We've seen that throughout hockey history, no matter how well or how poorly you're playing, when you're down a goal, you think we're one shot away. And that's what the Rangers did at that point.

"They were able to say, 'okay, everything we've done before now has been pretty awful, but it doesn't matter, because now we're one shot away and now we can play the way we've played all year and the way that made us successful all year. If we do that, we're one shot away from tying the game and maybe we can win it and go onto Game 7 as Messier promised.

"I think that it changed the tone of what the Rangers were thinking, of what the game felt like, probably what Marty Brodeur felt, he was just a kid then, and certainly the way the Devils felt about the way the Rangers were getting through their trap with their speed and creating some offense with their skill.

"It was a classic series, because, they say in boxing that styles make great fights -- opposing styles. And that's exactly what that series was. It was a team that was defense first and trapping and smothering against a team that just wanted to go, go, go and pressure the pocket; play with speed and play with skill. It was a brutal, vicious series, probably one of the most brutal I've ever seen. But it was also two contrasting styles and up to that point in the game, the Devils' style was clearly winning.

"Then in the third period Messier gets one to tie the game and gets another one for the lead. In the third period I remember Leetch, who was fabulous, for the last half of the game, with one arm taking the puck out of the zone and going past Bobby Carpenter and he got it over to Kovalev, who have carried in and found Messier, who was flying down the right side and Messier put a backhander along the ice past Brodeur. It was early, like 2:48 into the third period and now it's 2-2.

"Obviously that was the point that just wiped out everything that had happened to that point and now it's a 17 minute game with the Rangers' season on the line. Then you had that four-on-four, which was probably more popular back in those days. Those four-on-fours played to the Rangers' advantage. Leetch got it to Kovalev and Kovalev actually took a shot, a high, hard shot off Brodeur's arm and Messier just blew right past Bernie Nicholls.

"Ironically, Bernie was the guy who was traded to Edmonton to get Messier to New York. Now he was with the Devils and Messier just blew past him, knocked in the rebound and now it's 3-2 and everything's changed.

"Then, of course, Glenn Anderson, being Glenn Anderson, took a ridiculous penalty in the last minute -- a slashing penalty. I think it was Scott Stevens, or it might've been Bernie Nicholls, and it caused a little bit of a scrum for both teams -- kind of like a little line brawl, but not a fight. And, what it in effect did, was it gave Messier a chance to ice the puck with an empty-net, for his hat-trick, because of the penalty. There was no punishment for icing the puck.

"So Messier shot one, 150 feet into the empty net and he had his three goals and an assist. It was just a remarkable performance. Guys were raving about it from everywhere, all corners of the League, talking about how they'd never seen anything like that before; they'd never seen such leadership.

"He didn't need the third goal, but he got it. When he had two goals and an assist and they're up 3-2, you're saying, 'holy cow, can you freaking believe what we're seeing here? This guy made this promise and actually pulled it off.' He did probably what no other player in the league could've done at that point, just because his will was so strong, because he was a guy whose determination was unmatched and a guy who had built the trust, the respect and the admiration of all those guys; all of them, right down to the guys who weren't playing, like the assistant trainer and the guy who did their laundry.

"They were all pulled up by him all the time and now, you're saying, 'holy cow, he's actually doing this. He's actually going to pull this off.' And, of course, they still had a while to go. They still had some time to kill, still had to protect that lead. But 'holy cow' and 'holy crap' turns into, some other level of 'Holy Shit' when he scores the third goal. You see it when he goes back to the bench, he just leans into the bench and they're all going bonkers, patting him on the head and hugging him. It was just a remarkable performance given everything he did.

"For the second-half of that game, it was remarkable. He was being lauded as the greatest leader of all-time. And he hadn't been, to that degree, at that point; I don't think, even though he had five Stanley Cups -- he'd only been captain for one. I think that that really made him more of a legend than he was. People were saying some crazy stuff, like they had never seen a game like that by one player. They'd never seen anybody pull a team through a victory by himself like that. And, again, it wasn't honestly by himself. But what he did with three goals and an assist, after promising that, was remarkable.

"I do remember that Kenny Daneyko, who grew up with Messier in Edmonton, they were childhood buddies. And Kenny said that, in the second period he looked at Messier's face and Messier knew it was over. He thought it was over, because he didn't have any answers at that point. It was an interesting statement because, Kenny was as amazed by Messier's performance as anybody.

"But he also thought that Messier, at that point, thought it was over. And I think it's a remarkable statement. I do remember after the game too that Richter said, 'that which doesn't kill you, makes you stronger.' So they headed into Game 7 off of that, although it really didn't mean anything. It didn't help them or hurt them or affect Game 7 in any way, in which they obviously ended up winning.

"In the Meadowlands, the locker room was pretty small and cramped and I do remember that when the Rangers would play there, most of the time they'd kind of bring the players out one at a time. So I don't recall when Messier came out, at what point, but obviously you couldn't get near him. I remember he was kind of pushing the spotlight away from what he had just done and was more focused on what was coming up, which was obviously Game 7, which is a bigger game than the one they just played.

"So I don't even remember quoting him. I'm sure I did, but it wasn't, 'look what I just did.' It wasn't anything about the guarantee. It was more about; we're going to play the biggest game of our lives in two nights. But the other guys, their jaws were on the floor talking about Messier and his leadership, how they believed in him, how he believed in them and also so many guys just shaking their head saying they've never seen anything like that and probably never will.

"Some guys were saying there aren't many players in the game who could do that, and they pointed to 99 (Wayne Gretzky) and 66 (Mario Lemieux) as guys who maybe could do it, but had never done it. And there certainly haven't been many in the history of the game to do what he did, the way he did it, under those circumstances."

COMMENTARY FROM OTHERS AT THE GAME

MIKE RICHTER: "Well I just remember, heading into that game, you're playing against a great team. I think their record was the second best in the NHL behind ours. We may have beat Jersey every time we played them and that's what separated us. Those points mattered; so we had home ice advantage. We had played an emotional series against the Islanders, our crosstown rivals. It didn't matter the standings, it was going to be intense and we played well against them.

"Washington could be a dangerous team, but we closed it out in five. So we've played nine games, feeling good about ourselves, but knowing we were going to have a huge challenge in New Jersey. We lost the first game against New Jersey in double-overtime on a Stephane Richer goal. You understand when you're playing against anybody in the playoffs, they don't roll over and die for you, particularly when they're as talented and repetitive group as New Jersey was.

"So we weren't necessarily shocked there was pushback. There are games within a game and the momentum shifts each way; that's what great teams do. So, when we went down 3-2 in the series, there was a lot of drama surrounding who's playing, who's benched and who's starting, all that kind of stuff. So, I think it was a compelling story where you either have this win by the Rangers and maybe go onto slay some of those ghosts that have played you for 54-years, or you have an epic kind of collapse after winning the President's Trophy.

"So there's a good story being written in either direction and a lot of hype around it. When we got down in the series, it seemed to me that the story that was kind of being written was: oh, these guys are in trouble, Rangers that is. And clearly you're challenged, you're playing against a great team and they're pushing back and now they have momentum; they're ahead.

"But I didn't feel that going into that game (Game 6). We stayed in a hotel overnight. I remember coming out that morning to go to the game, the elevator door opened and it was Mike Keenan in the elevator. I walked in; we just looked at each other and smiled like we just started laughing, because there's nothing else to say. You can draw up any strategy you want, give any speech you want, but in the end you have to go out and play hockey; you have to perform.

"We both knew it and both felt it and both felt good about it, going into that game. But the game got started and we were having a rough go. The ice was a bit tilted, they were just very aggressive. They were pushing us. And we weren't responding. We didn't seem to be in sync as much as we could be. I don't think it was us playing particularly bad. It was them playing that good. They were a good team and all I could think of at the time was to weather the storm -- don't do anything radical, please don't pull me. I felt great.

"But I think, maybe it was (Claude) Lemieux, who tipped one in for the second goal. That second goal, at the time, we had gotten into penalty trouble. They were coming at us hard, but if we could just get through that and punch back a little bit we'd be okay. My big fear was Keenan was going to bench (Brian) Leetch or was going to pull me or put us in a position, where to get the team going, he was going to prove a point. But we didn't have much time.

"You have 60 minutes in your season, 50 minutes at that point; halfway through the first period at that point. We did call a timeout, but it didn't seem to stabilize things. That Rangers team had a lot of character and a ton of talent; but also game breakers. (Mark Messier) Mess had always said that about a guy like (Alex) Kovalev.

"You know if you're playing against the '94 Rangers, you're going to watch Leetch. You're going to watch Messier. You're going to have to watch (Sergei) Zubov. You're going to have to key in on a few guys like you always do. But we could beat you in so many ways and so, we were competitive in terms of being able to physically play a strong hitting game. We could skate well. We could shut down defensively when we needed to. We had the capability of scoring goals and that's precisely what happened.

"You know, you focus on Mark too long and the next thing you know, Alex -- I think it was at the end of that second period -- scored that goal. He just walked in and shot it, like it wasn't a big deal, not a big moment. He just made something of nothing, scoring on (Martin) Brodeur, who was playing great.

"Alex had that ability to be a game-changer and he was there. And that's what kept us within striking distance. We never got three, four goals behind. It was one, two. And that means, if you get a goal, you can be within reach of changing the momentum. And we did. You could feel that the momentum had changed throughout the game. It took some time, even through the end of the second period and into the third.

"We went into that third period with hope, more hope than we ended the first period with. It's so hard to change momentum on your side when it's against you. But I really felt that if we could weather the storm in that game and weather that game in the series, now the pressure is deeply on New Jersey. We were kind of cornered at the moment. We were close to death and a bit wounded, but they didn't kill us.

"Now we've already faced that and we're coming back, the series is even and that sets-up Game 7. To me, you'd already kind of gone through this and you just have to see how your team responds and we found out how our team responded. We won that game even though we were down goals in that game. And that takes a little bit of courage and sometimes luck. But we were able to kind of stare death in the eye and not blink and comeback. And so I felt even more confident going into the seventh game. But let's be clear, you're playing against a great team. They now have had two chances to eliminate you and we've really only had one chance to eliminate them.

"We'd worked all year to get that home-ice advantage, we had the home-ice advantage and the home-ice advantage does mean something. The Garden Faithful, they come, they are a beyond impressive group to play for and tough group to play against. Look, if you could set it up and say, you're in the Conference Final, at any moment of the year, where do you want to play? That's why you work so hard during the season to get that home-ice advantage.

"We had played them how many times in Training Camp? Six times during the season, six times prior to this game. We'd played those guys 14 times or so that year. I don't know if I have the numbers right, but there was a lot of hatred built up. We knew them well. We've scouted them. We've played against them. We've seen the changes they've made and they've adjusted to the changes we've made. It was just two teams that had to go out there and slug it out.

"You try to have the discipline of thought and just stay in the moment as much as possible. I can't score a goal. I can only worry about saving shots. That's my piece of the puzzle. And as you get older, across your career and across the season, you tend to get better at that. We've been practicing all year, our whole lives. This was like that driveway moment where you'd be outside, seventh game, sixth game, facing elimination, breakaway on you. What do you do in those moments?

"I look back now, Kevin Lowe had said something after they scored in the seventh game that did apply to the sixth game. So to fast forward, we were stunned when they scored with seven seconds left, but just to give you a little bit of perspective on this, he said, 'if it wasn't so hard it wouldn't feel so good when you did it.' And in some ways you'd tell, heading into the series, certainly as it got started and certainly by Game 6; this was a difficult series that's going to take everything our team had and everything their team had in order to come out with a victory.

"We were so well matched, so intense and seven miles away -- the two rinks -- or whatever the hell it was. The fans in both buildings, it just was a perfect matchup for two heavyweights to come together like that. Seeing Messier do that. I was a bit in awe when his third goal finally went in. But I was thinking more, 'what do I need to do?' Just don't think ahead. Don't think about the next shot. Just keep staying in the moment as much as possible, because I felt we could strike and get back into the game at any moment and if we can keep them off the board as much as possible, we'll be in range of taking the game over.

"By the third period we felt great. In some ways it was helpful, going into that last two minutes, I think we had a penalty against us. Messier takes the puck on his backhand, just wheels and shoots it all the way down the ice and it goes right in the middle of the net. We used to do that sometimes after practice just for fun. (Mike) Keenan would have us take the puck on one side of the defensive face-off dot, go around the net and just shoot it before you get to the second dot.

"Professional hockey players have practiced it their whole lives and we'd go through the whole team and maybe four guys would put it in the open net surprisingly. There was no pressure, we were just screwing around. It was just practice, it didn't matter. But in that situation, you don't want to miss the net. You don't want to have an icing. It's not as easy when you have someone trying to take your head off when you're going fast and your back is to the play.

"The puck was in the air, it landed somewhere near center ice and I'm just shaking my head saying, 'that son of a bitch, he called it. He's going to get a hat-trick, the game-winner. He called it, game-winner and hat-trick. It was just such an amazing sports moment. You can't script these things. Great players write these amazing stories. I do remember, the puck was still in the air and I'm shaking my head going, 'Oh My God, he did it!' It was just an awesome thing to be part of, for the team, the organization and the city. It was so cool to be a part of that."

MOST UNFORGETTABLE RANGERS MOMENT

RICK CARPINIELLO: "My first season was 1978-79 and I was only covering home games and occasional practices; we had another beat writer and I was helping them out. But that '78-'79 team, when they beat the Islanders in Game 6 of the semifinals at Madison Square Garden. And let's not forget the Islanders went onto win the next 19 playoff series; they were remarkable. So, we knew how good that team was.

"We didn't know they'd win 19 straight playoff series, but we knew how good it was and we knew what a big event it was for the Rangers to knock them off. The Rangers were not a very good team, but my memory from that is the guys streaming off the bench to a mug JD, John Davidson; but more than that, the noise.

"It is the loudest I've ever heard The Garden, including 1994. And including anything else that I've ever witnessed at Madison Square Garden. It was just deafening, the place was shaking. The guys talked about how the bench was shaking during the game. And it was start to finish, from warm-ups through a really long post-game, an eruption of noise.

"I remember that Mike Lupica called the place 'The Monster' in one of his columns that year. And I'll never forget that because it was 'A Monster,' and it was such a huge advantage. So was The Coliseum, but the Rangers won, I believe, two games at The Coliseum that series. And I believe the Islanders won one game at The Garden, if I'm not mistaken. But the place, that was my snapshot, how loud, how crazy that building was. Seeing Denis Potvin crumpled along the boards with his head up against the boards and Mike Bossy and (Bryan) Trottier, just devastated, while the place just exploded; that's my snapshot."

3 JOHN DAVIDSON (MSG NETWORKS)
GAME 7: 1994 STANLEY CUP FINAL (@MSG)
JUNE 14, 1994
NYR 3, VAN 2

BACKGROUND

"OH BABY!"

John Davidson's popular catchphrase was so beloved by fans that it helped land him in the NHL Hall of Fame; courtesy of the prestigious Foster Hewitt Memorial Award, which he received in 2009 for his exemplary work as a broadcaster.

But, long before Davidson's voice echoed through the homes and televisions of hockey fans everywhere, he was a goaltender in the National Hockey League.

Davidson's on-ice career spanned 10-years and two teams, the St. Louis Blues and the New York Rangers. And, while Davidson started his career in the city known as the "Gateway to the West," he is most remembered for his time in New York.

After making his NHL debut for the Blues during the 1973-74 season, Davidson went on to appear in 79 regular season games -- and one playoff game -- before being dealt to New York for the 1975-76 campaign.

It was in New York where Davidson began to make a name for himself, not with flashy numbers, but with sheer grit and determination. And those are two qualities Rangers fans loved about him. His unfortunate knack for suffering injuries was a big reason why his numbers weren't flashy and a big reason why his career ended after only 10 seasons. But it was his fierce competitive fire that fueled him to persevere. And Blueshirts fans everywhere rooted for him because they knew he would do everything in his power to deliver them victories.

In fact, Davidson practically willed his teammates to the 1979 Stanley Cup Final as he played through an injured left knee. Throughout that playoff season, the Ottawa, Ontario native compiled a .921 save-percentage, 2.28 goals-against-average and one shutout across 18 games. Not bad for a guy essentially playing on one leg.

Unfortunately, that proved to be the high-point of Davidson's goaltending career, as he never made it back to the Stanley Cup Final. At least, not as a player.

Following the 1982-83 seasons, which he played at the age of 29, Davidson's body could no longer handle the rigors of playing in the NHL, so he hung up his skates and transitioned into his second career; the broadcast booth.

"I retired at an early age," explained Davidson. "I was 29-years-old and I'd been a television sports junkie my whole life growing up in western Canada. As a kid, I would watch Hockey Night In Canada, so I just always wanted to do that. And then playing through injuries late in my career, even though I was still young, I was asked to do bits here and bits there and I really enjoyed getting into that. Then when I first retired with the Rangers, they allowed me to do some things with Madison Square Garden Network as the third man in the booth. I worked at it and I loved it."

"When you're that young and you're wondering what you're going to do the rest of your life, that's something that was there for me," said Davidson. "At least I could give it a shot. I decided to go in with both feet. I really worked at it and had a lot of help along the way, from some very good people, and it just grew and I loved every minute of it. It was outstanding. It took me around the world. I've been fortunate in my life; I've had three different transformations. One was a player, two as a broadcaster and three as a person in the front office. So I've been fortunate it's all under the same umbrella of hierarchy and it's now 45 years later."

Of the three transformations John Davidson went through, the first was how he built his connection with Rangers fans. But the second was one of the biggest love affairs ever seen between a fan base and a broadcaster. During his time with MSG Networks, Davidson spent most of his time teamed with Sam Rosen on Rangers telecasts. While Rosen delivered his patented style of play-by-play, Davidson brought a unique brand of color commentary. And the two worked together seamlessly.

So, when the 1993-94 season came along, it wasn't just the Blueshirts' players who had a tremendous season. Rosen and Davidson chronicled the franchise's most memorable season in 54-years. Therefore, it's no wonder that the game "JD" remembers best, is also the game that prompted Sam Rosen to announce to the world, *"And This One Will Last A Lifetime!"* And that's Game 7 of the 1994 Stanley Cup Final versus the Vancouver Canucks.

MOST UNFORGETTABLE RANGERS GAME

John Davidson wasn't born in New York, but that hardly matters. Rangers fan accepted him as a player and as a broadcaster to the point where he may as well be a true blue, New Yorker. And Davidson loves the fans and the city right back.

So, when the Canucks stormed back from a 3-1 series deficit to force a Winner-Take-All Game 7 in the 1994 Stanley Cup Final, it was only fitting that the adopted New Yorker was experiencing the same emotions as Rangers' fans everywhere.

"The tension in the building was special for the Rangers fans who were there," said Davidson. "It was great. You can't duplicate it because it was Madison Square Garden. It's just different. It's louder and more passionate than maybe anywhere I've ever been."

The Rangers had so much riding on that series; especially after their epic seven-game series against New Jersey in the Eastern Conference Final. After all, it had been 54-years since the Blueshirts had hoisted the Stanley Cup. 54 long, torturous years; during which time Rangers fans had been on one heck of a roller coaster ride of emotions.

There were the near-misses in 1950, 1972 and 1979. There were the disappointments of the early 1990s. But then came the magical 1993-94 season. The Rangers won the President's Trophy as the best team in the league during the regular season.

They followed it up with a sweep of the Islanders in the first-round and a five-game triumph over the Capitals in Round Two. The Devils had them on the brink in the Eastern Conference Final, taking a 3-2 series lead over New York into Game 6. But Mike Keenan's team found a magic more powerful than the so-called, "Magic Elixir," their 1950-51 counterparts consumed.

A "called-shot" hat-trick from captain Mark Messier saved the Blueshirts in Game 6. And mid-season pick-up, Stephane Matteau won Game 7 in double-overtime to send the Rangers to the Stanley Cup Final for the first time since 1979; a year in which, John Davidson backstopped his team to the cusp of greatness. Could his Modern-Day counterpart, Mike Richter, finish the job Davidson had started 15-years earlier?

Game One was dominated by New York, except for the fact that Vancouver's netminder, Kirk McLean stole the game for the Canucks; making an astounding 52 saves.

But New York wasn't deterred. And they proved it by winning three straight games to put them on the doorstep of a long-awaited championship.

"The thing that was interesting about that series was it could have been four straight," said Davidson. "That's how good the Rangers were those first four games. Kirk McLean stole one in New York, but it very easily could have been four straight."

With the Stanley Cup in attendance, the Rangers were primed to win Game 5 at home, in front of their adoring fans. But Vancouver had other ideas. A three-goal outburst from the Canucks quickly put New York's dreams of celebrating at home on ice. But a funny thing happened. The Rangers came back to tie the game with three goals in the span of roughly six minutes, a quarter of the way through the third period. But as quickly as they came back, they watched it slip away as Vancouver scored three more goals to send the series back to Western Canada for Game 6.

"Vancouver found a way to use their size and their fore-checking type of game to extend the series," explained Davidson. "And they deserved a ton of credit for that."

And just like they did in Game 5, Vancouver dominated Game 6, winning 4-1, to send the series back to New York for Game 7.

"It was almost a war of attrition because of the punishing style of hockey the Canucks played with," said Davidson. "Kevin Lowe and Sergei Zubov in particular were banged up. So Game 7 turned into an extremely close game."

So, after 54-years, a President's Trophy regular season, three rounds of playoffs and six grueling games with Vancouver the Rangers found themselves on home ice, in front of their most loyal fans; 60 minutes away from the prize that had eluded them for over half a century. Could they finally seal the deal?

Here's John Davidson on the call.

JOHN DAVIDSON: "It was a great hockey game. Remember, working for Madison Square Garden Network, you tried to be professional because it's your job. Sam was extremely excited. Al Trautwig was excited. Everybody was because how many times in your life when you cover a team for years and years and you get into one of those seasons where they win the President's trophy."

The Rangers got out to a quick 1-0 lead courtesy of a Brian Leetch goal. And they soon doubled their good fortune as Adam Graves added a power-play to put the Blueshirts up 2-0 in the first period.

JOHN DAVIDSON: "I also had a real true gut feeling they could win it all because I also went around and did a lot of games for other networks and saw all the other teams play. And I knew the Rangers, in my opinion, had a great chance to win the Stanley Cup because they were the best team in my mind. Now it's never easy to win and you get pushed and pushed, like the Devils pushed them, and the Canucks pushed them. But they did win, which doesn't happen very often.

"To take a magical run like that and get to the Stanley Cup Final, which the Rangers are in for the first time since 1979. Then, all of a sudden it looks like they're going to have a runaway and then it completely changes and the next thing you know, you're in a Game 7. So, you're in Game 7, covering the team you played for, covering a team you have watched and that you think is the best team. And they're playing at home in Madison Square Garden, with people who have been so loyal for so long, who wanted to win so bad."

With the Rangers' 2-0 lead still intact to start the second period, Canucks' captain Trevor Linden jump-started his team with a short-handed goal to cut Vancouver's deficit to a single goal.

JOHN DAVIDSON: "The game just didn't stop. As a broadcaster you didn't even have time to think about, what's next? It was just flying by and as an analyst I was just trying to do my job, not mess up and just stay in the moment. You've got a lot of people watching."

As John and Sam were trying to keep themselves composed, Mark Messier padded the Rangers lead with a power-play goal of his own to put the Rangers up 3-1. A lead they would take into the third period. And what a third period it was as Trevor Linden did his best to match Messier, scoring a power-play goal 4:50 into the third period to bring Vancouver within 3-2, with just over 15 minutes to go in regulation. And from that point on, the Canucks dominated the play, but Mike Richter stood tall -- with a little help from the goal posts.

JOHN DAVIDSON: "I remember there was a post hit by Nathan LaFayette and I just thought to myself, 'oh my goodness!' Then the Canucks kept their fore-check going. They were trying to punish the Rangers and force turnovers."

The Canucks kept on pushing, but Richter and his teammates weren't going to be denied. It seemed like the Canucks would just come in waves, but the Rangers netminder held his ground. And as the time on the clock ticked away, it became apparent New York was going to weather the storm. But not without a little last minute drama.

JOHN DAVIDSON: "I remember there were two icings in the final seconds of the game. And then came the final face-off. Steve Larmer pinned one of the Canucks against the glass behind the goal-line and then the game was over and everybody was jumping around. Meanwhile, Larmer still had his guy pinned against the glass; just to make sure. Then he released him and everybody was going crazy because the Stanley Cup was there."

The Rangers had ended their decades-long quest to win the Stanley Cup, in dramatic fashion. So all that was left to do was celebrate. But John and Sam weren't going to be so lucky. Or were they?

JOHN DAVIDSON: "Mike McCarthy was the Executive Producer and he made us go to The Garden to broadcast the parade out of the studio. And frankly, Sam and I weren't too happy. We wanted to be down there with the whole group and be a part of it. So as it starts, we're on set doing our jobs when in comes two of New York's Finest, as they essentially kidnapped us. They put us in a police car with the lights flashing and rushed us down to the parade to be a part of it.

"Evidently, it was all a set-up by Mike McCarthy, which actually turned out to be hilarious. We were happy to be 'kidnapped.' It was a special time and we got to see the whole thing."

COMMENTARY FROM OTHERS AT THE GAME

ADAM GRAVES: "There was a real benefit to us having that extra day off in between Game 6 and 7. Going across the country and being at home for Game 5, being down three goals and storming back and then they end up winning 6-3.

"And then we went back to Vancouver and the momentum had really shifted in their favor. We had a tough night in Vancouver and we lost 4-1. But, because we were a banged up team and obviously after that New Jersey series, which was such a physical battle all over the ice, it took its toll I think on every single player in our locker room. And I think by having that extra day off, back in the day you used to play every second day. And that was the rhythm of the playoffs, whereas the rhythm in The Final, and you're going from New York to Vancouver, and then back and forth.

"I do remember getting out on the ice for warm ups and hearing the chants of 'We Want The Cup,' and then not being able to hear John Amirante sing the national anthem and then hearing Frank Sinatra's 'New York, New York,' to start the game and the energy was palpable; it was just fantastic. Those are the things you hold near and dear to your heart.

"To a man everyone would tell you it was a gift and a privilege to be a part of that team, to be a part of the Rangers organization, to wear that jersey and be a part of that team in 1993-94. That bond is so strong; it gets stronger by the minute and by the day. And I think when you reflect back on it now, I know that the last two minutes of that hockey game were as long a two minutes as you're going to find.

"But it was the only way it could be after 54-years and all the things that had happened in the past. You knew it would be written that way, that the last couple minutes with the icings and the close calls and that it would be a nail biter to the end. That one last face-off was won and we all jumped on the ice; it was just like a dream come true. And certainly a dream come true to win in New York and win as a Ranger."

MOST UNFORGETTABLE RANGERS MOMENT

JOHN DAVIDSON: "I mean there was over 20 years of special moments in that place for me, being a part of Madison Square Garden Network. Seeing Steven McDonald being a part of the All-Star Game. Being a part of the seventh game. Being part of the Devils series. In the old days you had the Flyers and Rangers going after each other.

"Watching Brian Leetch grow up as a very young man and end up being in the Hockey Hall of Fame. We lived just about all of it. Seeing Mike Richter have his jersey retired in that building. Just the history of the Rangers and being a part of it, whether it is on the ice as a player or as a broadcaster in the booth calling games. Nothing ever is anywhere like Madison Square Garden."

4 STAN FISCHLER (SPORTSCHANNEL)
GAME 6 & 7: 1994 EASTERN CONFERENCE FINAL (@BRENDAN BYRNE ARENA, @MSG)
MAY 25, 1994; MAY 27, 1994
NYR 4, NJD 2; NYR 2, NJD 1 (2OT)

BACKGROUND

"The Hockey Maven," Stan Fischler, is known across the NHL as one of the brightest minds in the game. His nearly seven decades worth of experience, accumulated as both a writer and as a television analyst, are second to none; especially when it comes to the New York/New Jersey area.

Stan Fischler has authored over a 100 books, most of them hockey related, and has earned numerous accolades during his time covering the New York Rangers, New York Islanders and New Jersey Devils. Oh, and for the sake of accuracy, let's not forget about his stint broadcasting games for the Hartford Whalers.

While "The Maven," hung up his microphone following the 2017-18 season, he still keeps himself active as a prominent hockey historian for the NHL's website; consistently creating various forms of material for fans to learn about the great game of hockey.

But before he became "The Hockey Maven," he was just another kid from Brooklyn, New York, who was fascinated by the game of hockey.

"I went to my first game at The Garden in 1939, when I was seven," said Fischler. "And I instantly became enthralled with the game. But I was too young to go to the Rangers' games, so I went to the Rovers' games -- they had double headers on Sunday afternoons. The Rovers were really terrific. There were MET League games, which were local players. It was not limited by age and there were four teams: the Sands Point Tigers, Manhattan Arrows, The Jamaica Hawks and The Stock Exchange Brokers, who became The Brooklyn Torpedoes during World War II.

"There was a wonderful preliminary game at 1:30 and then at 3:30 the Rovers would play. The Rovers were the Rangers' farm team in the Eastern League. Just excellent hockey, exciting, I loved it. Rangers games at that time started at 8:30, so my parents wouldn't let me go because it was too late and I had school the next day. So I didn't go to a Rangers game until 1942.

"In '42, for my 10th birthday, my parents gave me a little Philco Radio, it was called the Transitone and a scrapbook with an Indian Head, a three dimension Indian Head on it. Those were catalysts for my love of hockey. With the radio, I was able to pick up Canadian games from Toronto, with Foster Hewitt announcing. He was very, very exciting, so I became a Leafs fan just by listening to him. To this day, there has not been an announcer to equal Foster Hewitt the way he did a game. There are a lot of wonderful announcers, but Foster was The Dean.

"With the scrapbook, I started to clip stories out of the papers, which, at that time, were just the New York papers. So in 1942, the clippings started. And this was all part of my hockey infatuation. I was an only child, so hockey was like my brother in a way. It gave me something to do. I still have every scrapbook, starting with 1942. It was a different type of hockey journalism. It wasn't as intense as it is now, but it was more fun.

"By the 1946-47 season, when I started High School, I was a crazy, crazy Leafs fan. So, I was down at Times Square going to see a movie at The Paramount with my friend Howie Sparer and while I was waiting for him I was standing at 43rd between Broadway and 7th, where the old Times building was. At the bottom there was an out of town newspaper stand. It was a big deal; there were papers from all over the country and Canada.

"While I was waiting for Howie, I saw there was a newspaper called The Toronto Globe and Mail, it was only a quarter. I picked up the paper, turned to the sports section and saw all these hockey stories that weren't in the New York papers. Of course, the main stories were about The Leafs. I was amazed. It was like I was discovering gold.

"That night, I went home and opened up to the Editorial page and saw I could subscribe and it wasn't that much. So I subscribed and everyday, one day after it came out, I was getting it in my mailbox; I was only getting The Globe one day late. The stories and the writing were wonderful. I found one particular columnist named, Jim Coleman, who I emulated in my head, because I loved his style. I had all his columns in my scrapbooks. I had one scrapbook for every year and it was all Leafs. That was the year they won their first Cup out of three in a row (1946-47).

"Now, I was old enough to go to the Rangers games, which I did. My friend Jimmy and I became season ticket holders -- End Balcony section 333, row E, seats five and six. Just wonderful seats at The Old Garden, the End Balcony. Before that, when I was going to the Rovers' games, I would get a program and it had a lot of white space and on the roster page there was also a lot of white space. So, at the end of every game, I'd write stories on my own, which, in retrospective, was an indication that I liked to write.

"When my teams won it was a wonderful story. But when my teams lost, it was the referee's fault. I couldn't write hockey in High School, I did very little writing in High School. When I got to Brooklyn College in 1950, we didn't have a (hockey) team, but we did have a soccer team and I got to write about them. Soccer was very big and it was a great experience. That, plus one journalism course, taught by Phil Leddy -- no relation to Nick Leddy on the Islanders -- was the professor and he had a profound influence on me.

"So, in 1951, the Leafs won their fourth Cup in five years. Bill Barilko scored the winning goal, he had been my hero. But then he disappeared in a plane crash -- him and another guy. They were heading to the fishing area in Northern Ontario when they disappeared. They didn't find them for 10 years.

"I remained a Leafs fan through the 1951-52 season, but by that time, Herb Goren had become the Rangers' press agent and he formed a Rangers' Fan Club. I went to the first meeting; they had a few players there. It was very exciting. And I said, 'wow, this is for me.' So, myself, along with two other guys -- Fred Meier, who I'm still in touch with (we played roller hockey together) and Jerry Weiss -- decided to put together a Fan Club paper -- The Rangers' Review.

"At that time, the PR guy, Herb Goren, who formed the Fan Club -- it wasn't fans who did it, it was the Rangers -- allowed us access to the players. The first guy we wanted to interview was Eddie Kullman and he was a good, tough, checking forward. A lot of the players, the day of the game, stayed at the old Belvedere Hotel, which was across the street from The Old Garden. So, me and Freddy went up, before Kullman took his pre-game nap and we interviewed him. He was wonderful. We couldn't believe it.

"Then, as the Fan Club grew, I stopped being a Leafs fan and I became a Rangers fan and I became the Vice President of the Fan Club. Gradually, with all the writing, I had access to all the players and The Garden; I was also going to all the Rovers' games. And I knew the guy who ran the Rovers. His name was Tommy Lockhart, who was also a business manager for the Rangers. So, one day, I went to Tommy and I suggested that I write a newsletter about the whole Eastern League. It was very important to me and it would cost them nothing. So he said do it and every week he'd distribute my stuff.

"So, when I graduated from Brooklyn College in 1954, that September, Herb Goren offered me a job in publicity, as his assistant. It was like the old cliché, like dying and going to heaven."

That assistant publicity job started The Maven's long, illustrious career in the New York hockey scene. And it's still going to this day.

So, since he can date his Rangers' career back to the 1954-55 season, it's only logical that Fischler would have his pick of memorable Rangers games to talk about. However, knowing The Maven the way I do, I shouldn't be surprised that he not only chose two games instead of one, but he also chose two Rangers games he covered while technically covering them from the Devils' side of things.

In case you need any further hints on which games he chose, here they are: Game 6 and Game 7 of the 1994 Eastern Conference Final between the Rangers and Devils. You see, at the time, Stan Fischler was covering Devils games as a television analyst for SportsChannel. So, while the Rangers' and Devils' respective MSG Networks crews did not travel to the visiting arenas, SportsChannel had their broadcasters at every game.

MOST UNFORGETTABLE RANGERS GAME

The 1994 Eastern Conference Final between the Rangers and Devils represented a seismic clash between the two best teams in the NHL that season (1993-94).

Throughout the course of the season the Rangers had proven they were superior to the Devils. Whether it was beating New Jersey in the pre-season or beating them all six times they played each other during the regular season, the Rangers always came out on top. That is, until the playoffs arrived.

By virtue of winning the President's Trophy as the league's best regular season team, the Blueshirts were afforded home-ice advantage throughout the playoffs. That meant that, if the Devils were to have any chance at knocking off the Rangers, they'd have to win at least one game at Madison Square Garden, a place that was supremely friendly to its' loyal tenants.

The Islanders couldn't find a way to win at MSG during the first-round of the playoffs. Ditto the Capitals in round-two.

So, as you can imagine, there were a lot of obstacles stacked against the Devils when the series started. And then that all went out the window in Game 1, as New Jersey's Stephane Richer beat Rangers' goalie Mike Richter in double-overtime to give the Devils a series-opening victory. Just like that, the Devils had ended the Rangers' dominance over them and proven they were not going to be intimidated by The World's Most Famous Arena.

Down a game heading into Game 2, the Rangers looked to not only pull even in the series, but to also remind the Devils that they weren't going to just let New Jersey walk all over them. And then the Blueshirts went out and did just that, winning the second game by the score of 4-0.

The series shifted to New Jersey for Games 3 and 4. And while Brendan Byrne Arena (Meadowlands) was not MSG, it didn't matter to New York as the Rangers won Game 3 in double-overtime to take a 2-1 lead in the series; thus proving they didn't need to solely rely on home-ice in order to win games.

But then the pesky Devils tied the series in Game 4, sending the teams back to New York for Game 5. And just like in Game 1, the Devils showed no signs of being intimidated by The Garden Faithful; handily beating the Rangers 4-1 and putting New York on the verge of elimination.

Could the Rangers go into New Jersey and save their season by winning Game 6? Or would the Devils prove to be the superior team?

"The Hockey Maven" was there and he brings a unique vantage point to this potential series-ending game.

STAN FISCHLER: "It's The Battle of The Hudson, Rangers vs. Devils and the Devils are leading the series 3-2 come Game 6 in New Jersey. Now, of course, the Rangers were favored to win the series by a lot and the Devils are on the cusp of a huge upset and I was working the game for SportsChannel, which, at that time, was a rival with MSG.

"Not to mention there was this great rivalry between the Devils and the Rangers. And that was the game that was preceded by the Mark Messier prediction; that they would beat the Devils. Now if you asked Mark Everson, the guy who wrote the story for The Post, I think he would be candid enough to tell you that he embellished the story, so that the Messier prediction was a lot less than it came out to be.

"We know that that's been journalism through years, but it was not an unabashed Messier announcing it. It was Everson doing his creative stuff to make it look like a big story, which it became. It became one of the All-Time hockey stories. And I'm not criticizing Mark for this, because those of us in the business have done it at one point or another.

"The point is that now, before the game, you've got this back page stuff and I'm doing the game; not play-by-play, but what amounts to analysis and between periods interviews.

"Back in 1993, my youngest son, Simon, was very, very ill with heart problems and he needed a transplant; he was in the hospital. And one day, at my request to Barry Watkins, who was the Press Agent, I told Barry, 'it would be nice if you could get some guys to come down here to visit. And on a Saturday morning when things were very low with us, Mike Richter and Mike Keenan came in within five minutes of each other. I'll never forget that. Keenan gave me a hug that I could still feel.

"So now, it's an hour or two before the game and all of a sudden Barry Watkins comes over to me -- I knew Barry when he broke in at The Garden -- and he says, 'the coach wants to talk to you.' I was like, 'why would Keenan want to talk to me at this point in time?' And Watkins goes, 'well Keenan wants to talk to you.' Now I'm trying to figure out what he wants to talk to me about. So, right next to the studio, there was an empty room. So I walk in and then Keenan walks in and I had no idea what this was all about.

"He sat down and what I figured out later was that he wanted to let off steam. He wanted to get away from all this and I was a friend. He went on about how the refs were this and that and he was just letting off steam until he got finished. It was just so rare, it had never happened to me before or since. And that's another reason why this was such a memorable game.

"So, the Devils go up 2-0 and Mike Richter is in goal for the Rangers. Meanwhile, Johnny MacLean, who was in his prime, came very close to making it 3-0; which at that time -- it was before I invented the expression 'the dreaded three-goal lead' -- that three-goal lead would have been pretty damn tough to overcome. And Richter makes a tremendous save.

"So, it's 2-0 well into the second period and Alexei Kovalev, who was really one of the underrated, all-time Rangers, came down the right side, he had a good shot and he beat Marty Brodeur. Now, since I was doing the Devils' games, I was thinking Devils, I'm not thinking Rangers it was such a good shot, which it was, but Brodeur should have had it. And that was the crack.

"Now, at the end of the period, I did an interview with Bernie Nicholls of the Devils. He was a really good player and very honest. So it was still 2-1 Devils when Nicholls came into the studio. And I remember this vividly because, of course, he was sweaty and in the interview his body language, as well as his verbal language told me, the Devils were done.

"Now, if you go back and check the interview you'll see what I'm talking about. But he looked tired. There were things he said which indicated they were losing it. I was stunned in many ways by his mannerism. It wasn't that he was giving up; he was saying the tide was turning.

"After he left, I thanked him, I remember I went to the washroom and all I could think, based on that interview, was the Rangers were going to beat them in the third period. I didn't know how, but then, of course, (Mark) Messier does his thing. But, as good as Messier was, that's how bad Brodeur was. Brodeur folded on the team in that third period. They needed the goalie to be at his best and steal it and he wasn't.

"So the Rangers tied the series and it was just a phenomenal series, with all the melodrama. Now it goes to Game 7, which in its' own way was equal to Game 6, in terms of the melodrama, the intensity and the fact that it looked like it was in the bag for the Rangers.

"Then the last face-off, Bill McCreary was the ref -- he just got inducted into the Hall of Fame -- and the Devils score, tying the game. I do have to add one important thing. When (Valeri) Zelepukin tied the game, Richter was irate. He came out, went behind the net and confronted McCreary. And there was contact; angry contact, yet not even a penalty was called.

"But anyway, we went to overtime and what I remember about the overtime, since I was doing the Devils' side, was that at one point, in the first overtime, Richter went behind the net and he was not the best stickhandling goalie.

"He went behind the net and Billy Guerin, who was coming into his own, goes behind the net and steals the puck from Richter. But he didn't have a good handle on it. If he would have had a good handle on it, he would have come out, around and put it in. But he didn't, so the Rangers escaped. That was the Devils' best chance.

"Now it goes into the second overtime and what killed me about the second overtime was that it was all Rangers. The Devils didn't get the puck. The Rangers would get into the Devils zone and if the Devils got the puck they'd throw it out to center. I was saying to myself, 'they just keep giving the Rangers the puck. And sooner or later, the Rangers are going to score.' And that's the way it went. On the winning goal, again, Brodeur was bad. What kind of goalie gives that up? It's short-side, it's an easy stop.

"But it started with (Viacheslav) Fetisov, who was an older defenseman and he was tired. The puck came out to center, the Rangers get it, regroup, get the puck in and bang the Rangers win the series. And, of course, like I said, I was very disappointed in Marty on that play, but it followed the pattern. Many years later, I asked Larry Robinson, who was the Assistant Coach then, I said, 'what the hell happened in the second overtime?' And he said, 'we ran out of gas.'

"After the game, I had to do the Devils' room, including Dr. (John) McMullen, who was the owner. It was just a very sad situation to be in. But it was part of the job. And it was a prelude to the Rangers winning The Cup. But those two games, they have to be together because it was the turnaround. The Devils come back, tie the game and then the Rangers turned it around."

COMMENTARY FROM OTHERS AT THE GAME

LARRY BROOKS: "I was covering the Devils for The Post, it was my first year back actually. For the Messier game, I actually covered the practice where he said, 'We'll Win,' and it didn't strike people as outrageous. It just struck me as a matter of fact and most of the people I think, who were covering it, as here was a guy on a team in trouble. They'd been outplayed badly the two previous games and he was basically just saying, 'hey, we're going to win.'

"But I was probably as surprised as Mark was to see it like that on the back page. It's probably the most famous back page in our history: 'We'll Win Tonight, Captain Courageous, We'll Win Tonight.' But I didn't leave there thinking that he had issued some sort of declaration that was a guarantee. I left there thinking he was the captain of the team that was going to lose and they knew it.

"(Mike) Richter won the series for them in Game 6. The Devils should have been up 4-0, 5-0; they dominated the first 36, 37 minutes of the game. And after it got to 2-0, they had at least six or seven glorious chances to make it three and then to make it four. When the Rangers scored towards the end of the second period, it was on a four-on-four when (Alex) Kovalev scored. It was clear that the entire dynamic had changed; the Devils had had their shot and didn't know how to put them away.

"The third period, of course, the Rangers, dominated. The Devils pulled their goalie pretty early at the time and Mark (Messier) scored the empty-netter. What I remember actually also about that day was I went to the Devils' morning skate and asked (Scott) Stevens if he cared to issue a guarantee of his own? But that wasn't his style and they were a little grumpy about it -- about the guarantee. But then they lost the game and they played two nights later at The Garden. And it was probably the best-played game I've ever seen in my life; for a game of that magnitude, for the Devils to play up to that level, two days after they had lost Game 6.

"It was a great, great game. (Brian) Leetch scored one of the great goals of all-time to go ahead, 1-0. Then obviously the Devils tied it was 7.7 seconds to go. I remember New Jersey had a couple of great opportunities to score in the first overtime and couldn't. And then (Stephane) Matteau scored, so it was probably the two best, most dramatic, back-to-back games, I've ever covered and that I think probably have ever been played in New York.

"It was the best I ever covered, either that or the 1979 series against the Islanders. It was history. I mean, it was history-making hockey. I don't think either team has played a series quite like that since. The Final in 1994 was pretty interesting. The Devils have had a few pretty interesting series too. But I think the pinnacle of New York hockey was the 1994 Eastern Conference Final."

MOST UNFORGETTABLE RANGERS MOMENT

STAN FISCHLER: "So I'm in the Rangers' publicity department; it's 1954-55. As I told you I had been a Maple Leafs fan. One of my favorite Leafs was a guy named 'Wild' Bill Ezinicki. He was the best body-checking forward in NHL history. I loved the guy. Eventually he went to the Bruins. So, as I said, in 1954-55 we didn't have a good team, a lot of things went wrong. And Ezinicki, by this time, was playing in the minors for Vancouver in the Western League. That was one of our two farm teams.

"We had a team in Saskatoon and a team in Vancouver. And, Ezy was called up in January or February. We were out of it already. The night before he gets called up, he gets into a fight in a game down there and breaks his thumb. But he comes up anyhow. There were two things that happened involving Ezy, because he was such a great body-checker.

"As a publicist, I had to come up with a gimmick to get a little ink. I got a hold of Dana Mozley, who was covering for The Daily News and had been there a long time, and I said, 'you know, you've got to watch

Ezinicki, because he's special.' He asked how? So I said, 'He has three types of body-checks. One is The Jolt. The second is The Thump and the best of all is The Whomp.' And he wrote this in his sidebar. I thought it was pretty clever to get some ink. And it got into print, so I felt pretty good about that.

"So now, they're playing the Canadiens -- '54-'55 -- and Rocket Richard is in his absolute prime. So, in my mind, what's Ezy famous for? His body-checks. So in this game, Ezinicki is on the ice against The Rocket. I'm in the press box and, of course, when Ezy is on the ice I'm focusing on Ezy, so The Rocket is coming out of his end -- on the right-wing -- and one of Ezinicki's styles in those days was he'd be very unobtrusive. And then he had a way of being like a sub with a torpedo.

"The Rocket was cutting to center and as he's cutting to center, Ezinicki pulls his swerve and, in my mind, this was the body-check that would kill The Rocket. It was so perfect the way it was lined up. I just couldn't believe, in fact, in a way, I was feeling a little bit sad for The Rocket, because you know, who wants to see Babe Ruth get beamed? So, just as Ezy was about to level him, The Rocket, it was like the story of The Titanic. The Titanic tried to avoid the iceberg.

"They saw the iceberg but they didn't manage to avoid it. So, The Rocket picked him up on his radar at the last second and it was like Ezy missed him by a quarter of an inch. And then The Rocket kept going. But I always thought, 'what would have happened if he had delivered that check?' It was such an exciting moment for me because he (Ezinicki) was my guy and now he was with the Rangers. Plus, I had given Dana Mozley, 'The Jolt, The Thump and The Whomp. And this would have been The Whomp. It was just one of my favorite memories."

5 JOHN GIANNONE (NY DAILY NEWS)
GAME 7: 1994 EASTERN CONFERENCE FINAL (@MSG)
MAY 27, 1994
NYR 2, NJD 1

BACKGROUND

Out of all the people who cover the Rangers, John Giannone might have the best office; for he is usually stationed between the benches during games. And in Giannone's own words, "they (the network) don't use me in the same way other networks use people, because I am the only guy who is between the benches in the NHL who never either played or coached. So I don't bring a player's or a coach's perspective. I bring a reporter's perspective, so every time in between the benches, I try to remember that."

Since, the Rangers already have a "Voice of the Team" in Sam Rosen, I felt it appropriate to give John a nickname as well. And after going through several options, he decided he's the "Heightened Senses of the Rangers." The nickname may take awhile to catch on, but it fits. Giannone's role between the benches means he hears and sees everything going on with the team throughout the course of the game. That, along with the propensity for pucks to fly his way, thus causing him to constantly be on high alert, is why he is the "Heightened Senses of the Team."

John Giannone comes from humble beginnings, as he grew up in Flushing, Queens, and he was exposed to professional sports at an early age. One day, his Father, who was an architect, was down in Philadelphia and bought young John a Flyers' jersey, which led to John idolizing Flyers' legend, Bobby Clarke. In fact, Giannone once sent away for signed pictures of Clarke and when he received them, it was as if Christmas had come early. Too bad his Mother made him rip all the photos to shreds as a punishment for the slightly misleading way he obtained the autographs.

But as John matured, he began to focus on a career in journalism. And that took him to Fordham University in The Bronx, where he made academic history as the only student to ever receive an A- from "The Hockey Maven," Stan Fischler. (To this day, it is the highest grade "The Maven" ever gave during his tenure as a college professor).

From there, Giannone began his newspaper career as a clerk for The NY Post in 1988.

"My career in newspapers began as a clerk in 1988 at the New York Post," said Giannone. "Basically, I would put box scores together and handle horse racing results. So I started at the very bottom; this after having worked at CBS Sports for a couple of years as a statistician and a researcher. Within a year or so I had kind of put in my name that I wanted to do some writing and they gave me an opportunity covering high school. Then my first beat was the Islanders, who I covered in 1990. From there I did the NY Jets in 1991, the NY Giants in 1992-93 and the Mets in 1994.

"But then, in April of that year, I'd say probably about April fifth," recalled Giannone. "I got a call from The Daily News saying that all three New York hockey teams were in the playoffs that year and they wanted to move Frank Brown from Rangers beat writer to columnist and let him cover the whole New York hockey story. So they were looking for a general assignment reporter who could start by just being the Rangers beat writer and writing all the game stories and covering them everyday; starting with the first playoff game. I said, 'sign me up.' My first assignment was the Rangers first playoff game against the Islanders. So I ended up covering the Rangers run right through to them winning the Stanley Cup."

Eventually, John made his way to MSG Networks in 2002 as an anchor at the sports desk. And after the 2004-05 season was cancelled due to lockout, the powers that be at the network decided they wanted to make an addition to the Rangers' broadcasts, so Giannone was brought on to conduct interviews between periods and to work the room during the post-game. Then, in 2012 he was placed between the benches for the first time, and minus some occasional stints in the radio or television booths, he's been there ever since.

In Giannone's tenure covering the Blueshirts, he has witnessed a number of magical games and moments. And just like his colleague Sam Rosen, John's most unforgettable game is Game 7 of the 1994 Eastern

Conference Final vs. New Jersey. But unlike Sam, who called the game on television, Giannone was a young beat writer for the New York Daily News, so he had a different vantage point for the game. And because of that, John's recollection of the game is rather different from Rosen's.

MOST UNFORGETTABLE RANGERS GAME

There are two words in sports that carry an added sense of excitement and drama. And they are: Game Seven.

Whether you watch baseball, basketball or hockey, Game 7 is the ultimate -- often epic -- conclusion to a playoff series. And it's made all the more dramatic when two blood rivals, who have been tearing each other limb from limb for six games, are forced into the winner-take-all situation.

So, when six games between the Rangers and Devils wasn't enough to determine a Stanley Cup berth, the two archrivals met in Game 7 to finally settle the score.

What ensued was nothing short of arguably the greatest playoff game ever played.

Here's John Giannone with the riveting tale.

JOHN GIANNONE: "The morning of (Game 7), I remember there were still mixed feelings from a Rangers' fan standpoint. It was just, chronicling what was happening in the city and the euphoria of what had just happened. Mark Messier had guaranteed victory and then backed it up with a hat-trick. He had rallied his team from a 2-0 deficit to win Game 6 on the road when everything looked like it was against them. Being down two goals in the second period and to score a third period hat-trick was one of the great individual feats, probably the single greatest feat, I've ever seen.

"I was there when he guaranteed victory. I looked at Vinny DiTrani from the Bergen Record, who was covering that day and we looked at each other. As soon as the press conference, or rather, press scrum was done -- it wasn't even at a podium, it was just Mark standing in the locker room -- we said 'he just guaranteed victory,' and we basically agreed that was the case and we went off and wrote it as such. And by that night it was splashed all over America.

"The euphoria of what he accomplished was mixed with the dread of, if we don't win then what he accomplished is just going to be a footnote in another playoff season of failure for the Rangers. I remember going up to the morning skate and it was still all the buzz, which was especially prevalent on the radio. So, the morning skate was at Rye

Playland up in Westchester County and there was a real workman like sense from the Rangers that, they had a job to do.

"The way Mark described 'The Guarantee,' it was like a business trip to New Jersey and they treated it like that. Then, it was time to take care of business that night. It was a warm, sunny day, but there was just a really weird vibe around the city about what we were going to see that night. Remember, it was two days after 'The Guarantee' and it was still what everybody was talking about.

"Now, here we are Game 7. I remember going to the morning skate and then making my way down to The Garden to begin writing. At the time -- I think newspapers still do this -- you would write an early story that basically holds the spot in the newspaper where the game story is going to go. That early story goes in the newspaper that gets printed and is then sent everywhere around the country.

"So, there are newspapers from the next day, May 28th, 1994, that don't have anything about Game 7 because those papers were printed before the game was ever played. I wrote that early story and it was basically just about the emotion as a beat writer. It was pre-internet, but everybody could still kind of find out what went on in the game before the next day's paper came out.

"For me, it was always about trying to portray the emotion, trying to bring the human element into my writing. At the morning skate a lot of the talk was about the emotion of it and just how, if they don't finish the job they extended two nights earlier, than it will all just have been a disappointing waste.

"Now, getting into the game, I remember the national anthem being sung by John Amirante and you couldn't even hear him singing; that's how loud the building was. I also remember from the minute the Rangers got on the ice for their skate half an hour before the game, the buzz was like nothing I'd ever heard before; and I had covered every playoff game to that point. That night brought the decibel level to a completely different place than I had experienced before.

"I could remember watching the 1979 Stanley Cup Final, Rangers vs. Canadians, Game 3 when it came back to The Garden tied at one. And I remember Billy Joel sang the national anthem and you couldn't hear him down on the ice. For Game 7 against New Jersey my seat was in the press box right above where the Zamboni came on and off the ice, which was just over the left shoulder of Marty Brodeur.

"As I recall, the Rangers scored early on an unbelievable play by (Brian) Leetch on a spin-o-ramma move, down below the goal line; 350 feet away from where I was. Leetch took it off the point and made a beeline toward the net, kind of around the left side, and looked like he was going to take his speed completely around the net, but he did a spin-o-ramma and just put it in the net. Brodeur didn't know where the puck was at the time and he didn't know where Leetch had gone. It was a remarkable goal and it caused the noise level in the building to go to an even higher level; one I had never heard before.

"From there, it just became a game of attrition. I mean, there were guys, I remember distinctly that Alexei Kovalev looked like he was never going to play the rest of that game after the injury he took. He went to the bench and was doubled over in pain. I remember Bobby Carpenter had to be helped off the ice by one of the Devils' trainers because of an injury he sustained.

"There was so much going on in the game, and if that game was played today, there probably would have been 20 penalties. That game had two; one in the second period to the Devils and one in the third period to Kovalev, when he took an elbowing penalty, which brought a sense of doom to The Garden that hadn't been felt before, not even after they had gone down three games to two at home.

"One of the things I remember too, was as those final minutes we're counting down, the chants of 'Defense,' and you never hear that at a hockey game. I mean, again, the Knicks were on just as magical of a run as the Rangers were at the time. They were involved in the Eastern Conference Final trying to beat out the Indiana Pacers to get to the Finals. Of course, every time the Pacers had the ball, chants of 'Defense,' would resonate from The Garden.

"It's a distinct voice which comes from this building and always has when it comes to basketball. But to hear it at a hockey game is so weird, especially when you consider that pucks are usually 50-50 propositions. But the Rangers fans understood, if we're going to win this game, we're going to win it 1-0 and we're going to win it on the back of our defense and our goaltender.

"I remember much of the last five minutes, that chant of 'Defense.' Every face-off the chant was 'Defense.' Any commercial timeout; it was 'Defense.' It wasn't even, 'We want the cup,' because they weren't even there yet. They still had to get through these final few minutes and I remember there were a couple opportunities for the Rangers to score and they didn't convert.

"And then I take myself right to 'that' face-off. There were 14.7 seconds left on the clock and then there was about a two-minute delay while the referees tried to figure out if more time needed to be added. All I can remember thinking was, 'this is going to give this Devils forward group, which had been out there trying to score with an empty net, a chance to get a little breather and to get a little rest; maybe even to formulate a play.

"It seemed like it took forever and then they got back to the face-off circle, after adding two seconds to make it 16.7. They dropped the puck, and remember, it's at the complete other end of the ice; I'm looking straight down the barrel at what's going on. They dropped the puck and Messier won the face-off. It kind of went behind him in the face-off circle, to the right of Richter, and to the left of where I was watching. Jeff Beukeboom came over and slapped it as hard as he could around the boards, but It didn't go very far because a Devil stepped up and stopped it. A Ranger went over and met him and it was a one-on-one battle. All the while, the clock is running down and the crowd is going berserk. You couldn't hear anything other than the deafening noise of the crowd.

"Claude Lemieux got the puck in the corner and Beukeboom, who had slapped the puck around the boards, looked like he was going to go around, to Richter's left post, but instead, made a beeline for the puck. Now you had Leetch to the right of Richter and you've got Beukeboom in the corner with another Ranger, which left Richter's left post completely unprotected. Lemieux threw the puck at the net and Richter stopped it. Then, Zelepukin is all by himself, just to the left of Richter, at the left post. He whacked at it the first time, but Richter made a kick save. But Zelepukin whacked at it a second time and this time it pops up and goes into the net.

"The clock actually should have read about 8.3, but it counted down to 7.7, where it finally froze. The groan in the building was actually drowned out by the screaming that I heard from people around me, who couldn't believe the puck went in. I remember, the first visual that stands out more than any other, is Mike Richter getting up and bum rushing, Bill McCreary, the referee and pinning him right into the boards.

"And I can still remember turning to John Dellapina, who was the Devils' beat writer at the time and who was sitting to my left, and I said to him, 'he's (Richter) going to get a penalty. He's going to get thrown out of the game and there's going to be overtime and the Rangers are going to have to play Glenn Healy.' To Bill McCreary's great credit, he understood the emotion of the moment. And to Mike Richter's great credit, he understood that he might have just crossed a line. He (Richter) backed off but continued to scream; to no avail.

"The Devils had tied the game. They went to center ice, dropped the puck and the last 7.7 seconds ticked off and they went to overtime. Meanwhile, that phrase about being able to hear a pin drop, you could have heard a feather drop in The Garden when that buzzer sounded at the end of 60 minutes. And I remember watching the broadcast and seeing graphic which read, 'Mike Richter, 102:11, shut out.' That meant he hadn't allowed a goal in 102 minutes and 11 seconds.

"I later came to find out that, Gary Thorne had talked about a statistic that it would be the first time ever that a goalie would finish with five shutouts in a playoff season, because he already had four between the series against the Islanders, the Capitals and the Devils. While we were still waiting to finish out the game, they (ESPN) were speaking of shutouts and then Zelepukin scored to send it into overtime.

"I remember, during intermissions we would leave the portal box and we would walk back to the press room to get a soda, a water or whatever, and maybe continue to write. Ours are running stories of what's transpiring and I remembered I waited a little bit in the portal box because I wanted to look around the crowd and get some visuals that I could put into writing. During the intermission, between third period and first overtime, the body language of Rangers fans, they were slumped in their seats with their heads in their hands, staring blankly. Every once in a while one guy would punch a wall and there was a whole lot of screaming expletives.

"Grief is probably the strongest word I could use. There was grief in the stands because Rangers fans, who hadn't seen the ultimate success in 54 years, truly believed when Zelepukin scored -- a Devil of all people -- that they were cursed and anything that just happened in front of them was proof positive they were cursed. I remember going back and writing some of that when I made my way back to the portal box, and when the Rangers came on the ice, there was a certain noise level, but it wasn't the same as the third period or the second period and certainly not the first period. It almost was the underlying sense of worry as much as the underlying sense of excitement and encouragement for the home team."

Just as Rangers fans were going through their roller coaster of emotions, so to were the reporters covering the game. And, as the first overtime began it was up to the Rangers to prove they could overcome the devastating ending to period number three. But just as the Blueshirts were beginning to push the pace, the Devils did their best to stop the hearts of every single fan inside Madison Square Garden, as well as those watching at home.

JOHN GIANNONE: "I remember a puck that hit off of, I believe it was Bernie Nicholls' skate, and it skidded toward the net; it just went wide. Again, I turned to John Dellapina and I said, 'could you imagine if this thing goes in off a skate?' And, especially when you consider that it was really the Rangers carrying the play through the game and through the overtimes. I believe the final shot totals were like 48 to 32.

"I mean Martin Brodeur made 46 saves in that game and it ended up being 2-1. So you know, the shot on goal totals and the puck possession totals would tell you the Rangers certainly dominated the play, but the Devils had their opportunities. There was a play in the first overtime where Richter came way out of the net and barely got back, almost giving it away for what would have been a 30 foot open net. You could hear people gasp and scream, 'NO,' at the same time.

"Then there was a play in the second overtime, just before the Rangers scored, where, I want to say it was Claude Lemieux, took a shot. Richter threw his arm up, made a glove save and the puck fell right at the top of the crease. (Sergei) Zubov was there, as was Nicholls and it's a miracle that Bernie Nicholls didn't get there first. It would've just been a tap in. I also remember, at the other end of the ice, I believe it was the second overtime, there was a shot from the point by Beukeboom, it might have been (Adam) Graves, and it was stopped by Brodeur and the puck just fell straight down, right onto (Mark) Messier's stick.

"He was all by himself. All he had to do is elevate it and the Rangers would go to The Final. He elevated it and Brodeur threw up his arm and made a save. It was at that point that I started to think, 'I don't know when this is going to end, or certainly not how.'"

There's an old adage in sports, that it's always going to be the person you least expect who comes through in the biggest moment. So, when Messier didn't end the game, it gave one of his teammates the chance to step out of his shadow. The questions were, who would it be, when and how?

JOHN GIANNONE: "The first thing I remember about (Stephane) Matteau, is talking to him after the game. And I remember him telling me the whole story, because I went back in the archives and looked at it. In fact, I wrote about it. His lace was broken on his skate and he didn't know it until he was lacing up his skates to go out for the second overtime. He went to tie his skates and the lace was broken. So he had to take his skate off and put a whole new lace in.

"When the second overtime began, Matteau was not on the Rangers' bench, he was in the dressing room. Only the Black Aces, the players who were scratched from the lineup, were in there with him and one of them was Eddie Olczyk. He said to Eddie Olczyk, 'bring me some luck.' So Olczyk grabbed his stick and kissed the stick blade. And I remember Matteau telling me when he got out of the dressing room; the NHL had moved the Prince of Wales Trophy between the locker rooms.

"In The Garden, before it was renovated, you had the Rangers' locker room as you walked off the ice to the right and the Devils' locker room down the hall to the left. And right down the middle in that corridor, between the dressing rooms, was the Prince of Wales Trophy; ready to be easily brought on the ice when a goal finally went behind one of the goaltenders.

"I remember Matteau telling me after the game, and I wrote about it, that he actually touched the trophy for good luck. Which when you think about it now is richly ironic because people don't touch the trophy when they win it because it's supposed to bring bad luck. But the ultimate good luck was brought to a guy who touched it before he went on the ice for that second overtime."

With Matteau's skate all fixed, he made his way to the bench, having made a decision that flew in the face of decades worth of superstition. So there he was, late to the second overtime, but on-time to become a legend.

JOHN GIANNONE: "Keep in mind, it's his first shift. He hadn't skated at all in almost half an hour thanks to the intermission and then having to get his skate fixed. So his legs were a little bit fresher perhaps. And what I remember about the play is (Viacheslav) Fetisov got the puck almost right in front of his bench and he went to pass it across the ice to (Scott) Niedermayer.

"It hit off a skate, I think it was Esa Tikkanen's skate, who was providing a little bit of a fore-check, and it caromed back and caught Niedermayer flat footed. And, because Matteau had just jumped on the ice, he had a full head of steam from the far bench and he just made a mad dash for the puck and he got to the puck about a half a step before Niedermayer did. He poked it past him and it banked off the corner boards and he grabbed it.

"Now, when he grabs it, he's got a half-step on Niedermeyer, who's now following him. As Matteau starts to go behind the net, Niedermeyer realizes, 'I'm not going to be able to catch him,' so he literally fish hooks him. He took his stick, put it right in his right arm and pulled back. He almost looked like he was water skiing, and today it absolutely would have been called a hook.

"I mean the goal still would have counted, but there was no penalty that was going to be called. But because he yanked back, that caused Matteau's body to actually turn to where his chest was now facing the ice. Perhaps Matteau had planned on a wraparound the whole time. Or, perhaps he was going to continue on along the boards. But that little tug pulled him into a position where the only thing he could do with the puck, was throw it in front and he threw it in front.

"Brodeur went down with his paddle and it hit off his stick and it popped up in the air and slid right between his legs. I just remember, there's a famous photo that hangs at the Rangers' practice facility in

Westchester today, and it's a huge blown up picture of the exact moment that the puck is on the blue paint, behind Brodeur in the net and Matteau realizes it and his arms are just going up and in the very upper left corner of that photo is me and John Dellapina.

"We were sitting there watching and Dellapina's arms started going up as well, not because he was rooting but because he could not believe that that puck actually got past Brodeur, because there was no way that that puck was going to go in. And then I just remember the bedlam. It was bedlam. I remember Zelepukin was on the ice and he tripped Tikkanen twice as Tikkanen was trying to get to the sideboards to join the celebration.

"The first guy there was (Steve) Larmer. The second guy there was Beukeboom and Tikkanen couldn't get there because he kept getting tripped by Zelepukin, as the Devils we're starting to realize that, 'Oh My God, we just lost on a wraparound.' Now remember, this is the same Matteau, who had scored in double overtime earlier in the series to win Game 3 for the Rangers and he scored in the most unlikely fashion against the goalie, who played out of his mind that night in stopping 46 out of 48 shots.

"Then I remember, just uproarious hugs. I remember looking at the Rangers' bench and seeing those Black Aces. It was Olczyk, Mike Hartman, Alex Karpovtsev and (Mattias) Norstrom. Their suit jackets were on backwards, inside out, that was their version of a rally cap. They actually took their suit jackets, turned them inside out and wore them that way. They were wildly celebrating on the Rangers' bench.

"And then I remember, the Rangers lining up, they had done their celebrations at the far end of the ice where they had mobbed Richter and Matteau, and going to the center line to start the handshake process. Meanwhile, the Devils were still standing, gathered around their 20-year-old goaltender who was hysterical crying.

"It had taken that long for them to compose themselves to the point of getting to the handshake line. They got to the handshake line and I remember watching vividly as Matteau and Brodeur shook hands. They just nodded to each other, probably said one word to each other in French and that was it. Then the Rangers peeled off, they brought the Prince of Wales Trophy out and Messier gestured to his team to come over and take a picture. Nobody skated around.

"And the only thing you heard in the building was, 'We Want The Cup, We Want The Cup.' That chat went on for 10 minutes. I think I wrote three or four stories that night from various perspectives. One of the last things I remember is being in the portal box and looking down, about 45 minutes after the locker rooms had emptied, and Broder and his girlfriend were standing at the Zamboni door just staring at the crease; staring at the spot where he had just allowed the most devastating goal a goalie could allow. And I remember I had to get that in my story and that was one of the things I wrote about before I left that night.

"We walked outside The Garden and I can remember it was as though they had won the Stanley Cup. I mean, the celebration that night could rival the Stanley Cup celebration because it meant the dream was still alive. Now it's funny, because I have watched video of the ESPN broadcast and Gary Thorne, again they kept showing during those last seconds of regulation, the banner that said 1940 up on the wall. And I can remember distinctly when Matteau scored the goal, one of the things Gary Thorne said is, '1940 is no more,' and I was like, 'no, that's not necessarily true.' But it sort of felt that way that night."

COMMENTARY FROM OTHERS AT THE GAME

JOHN DELLAPINA: "So actually, I can tell this from a different perspective because I was the Devils' beat writer that year. That was the last year of six years that I covered the Devils as a beat. I was with the Devils throughout that playoff series and then obviously The Final with the Rangers. We all know what happened in Game 6 and at practice the next day I went to Scott Stevens and said, 'why doesn't he just guarantee Game 7?' But that just wasn't done back then. Now, people do it as a matter of reflex. He just wouldn't do it. He was like, it's not me. He was supremely confident, don't take this the wrong way, I mean, the Devils fully expected to win that game. So, losing Game 6 was definitely a shock to their system.

"We all have different memories. (In Game 6) the Devils were killing the Rangers; I mean blowing them onto the Turnpike. And Mike Richter single handedly kept the Rangers in the game. I mean it was 2-0, but it should have been 6-0. Richter was just phenomenal and then the Devils made a bad line change and (Alex) Kovalev scores a late goal at the end of the second period and everything changed. The Devils thought they were fine, they felt like they were in The Final and suddenly they're in Game 7 at The Garden. And to their credit, they played the greatest game I've ever seen in person. They and the Rangers played the greatest hockey game I've ever seen in person and I've been blessed to see a lot of games in my life. It was amazing to me that they got off the mat and played the way that they played in that game.

"Brian Leetch scored an early goal to make it 1-0 and from that point on, both teams had a lot of chances, but it was still a 1-0 game. To this day, I maintain that Brian is my favorite player of all-time. And I don't think there's any argument he's the greatest Ranger and greatest American-born player of all-time. In some perfect cosmic universe, that goal should have been the only goal in the greatest game ever played, because it was an unbelievable goal. Brian drove down from the point, and did a spin-o-ramma at the post and tucks it in on the guy who became the winningest goaltender in NHL history. And I've spoken to Bill Guerin, who says to this day, 'Brian should have been the only person to score a goal in that game.'

"So, you're writing on deadline and then, with 7.7 seconds left Zelepukin does what Zelepukin does, and the building goes into complete shock. It was supposed to be a celebration at that point for the Rangers. They were finally going back to The Final for the first time since 1979. And then it's just horror. It's like, is this '72 with Ratelle breaking his ankle again? Or like (Denis) Potvin hitting Ulf Nilsson in '79. It's, 'are they ever going to win?'

"Then it becomes two extra periods of sheer terror. And you have the famous moment, which Sam Rosen captured so beautifully, when the puck is laying in the crease and John MacLean looks like he can jam it right in. And then Sam yells, 'where's the puck?' That's what the whole game was and that's what the whole overtime was. I know John (Giannone) has referred to this, we were sitting at different ends of that tiny press box that was over the Zamboni entrance; and it was an unbelievable privilege to watch those games from that perch. We're 15 feet from each other, calling each other on the phone every five minutes saying, 'how great is this?' As we were watching it, we knew we were seeing something unbelievable. And we would never see again. It was just amazing. When Matteau scored, we were 20 feet from it.

"If you grew up when we grew up, I don't want to tell you my birthday (chuckles), but whatever, we were Rangers fans. There was only the Rangers when we were growing up. The Islanders came when I was 10-years-old. You're not rooting for them (the Rangers) because you're too caught up in what you're doing (covering Game 7), but you know; I was with the Devils for seven months. I was with the Rangers for 30 something years as a kid growing up. So you're watching this and it's just amazing. It's right there. It's Messier and it's Leetch and it was unbelievable."

With the Rangers carrying a 1-0 lead late in the third period, it looked like the New York sextet was finally going to go back to the Stanley Cup Final. But the Devils had other ideas. And it was all thanks to a questionable whistle by the referee.

JOHN DELLAPINA: “I will say, with all due respect to my good friend Mike Richter, and he is a good friend of mine; Mike Richter playing the puck was never a good thing and he would admit to this. So, if I'm a linesman or a referee and I have a whistle, the last thing I expect is for Mike Richter to play the puck. Martin Brodeur, totally different circumstance. I have no doubt that Michael was trying to play the puck and keep it moving. But you know, if you're a referee and you've worked with Mike over the years, you expect him to hold that puck. And the Rangers were great on face-offs too. And by the way, it becomes a better story anyway. I’m sure Mike didn’t want to give up that goal but it becomes a better story.

“It's the far end of The Garden. It's at the Seventh Avenue end and we sat at the Eighth Avenue end. When you're writing, you're watching and you're intense, but you also have two thoughts in your head. One is, ‘when do I press this button?’ (Send and the story goes in.) It wasn't like the Devils were coming and coming. The Rangers kind of had it under control.

“The whole game was mayhem but it didn't feel like they were holding on for dear life. And then a couple of guys lost their men and Zelepukin, who was a nice journeyman player -- he wasn't Bernie Nicholls -- he scores this goal and Michael, who, he wasn't as placid as Brian, who was the most calm, placid player in the history of the National Hockey League, but he didn't do that kind of thing; he went bananas. When you look at the replay, a lot of Rangers lost their guy and I think a lot of guys on the Rangers, if they were strapped to a lie detector would say, ‘they were already celebrating at that moment.’ They didn’t exactly take care of business down the stretch.

“There’s a great story, not from the game, about John Campbell, the legendary harness racing driver, who at that time had more harness racing victories than anybody. Campbell was a gigantic hockey fan growing up outside of Toronto. So, he was taking a horse to the post as time was running out at the Meadowlands that night. And somehow, the game was on the scoreboard in the center of the track and he tried to delay the race so he could watch the final seconds cause he was a gigantic Devils fan. Finally, the Steward of the Outriders said, ‘John, you going to scratch this horse or we going to start this race?’ He said he couldn't wait to get around and that he has no memory of the race. He just wanted to get around to find out how the game ended. And then he had two overtimes to watch.

“Getting back to the game, I’ve worked at the NHL for 10 years now and I've gotten very close to a lot of referees. And that was not the time to throw Richter out of a playoff game. It just wasn't and also it wasn't an egregious thing. He wasn't trying to tackle the referee. He was jumping up and down and got too close and I think our referees know how to show discretion and they did at that time."

Jumping ahead to overtime, both teams had chances to end the game -- as well as the series -- but both goaltenders came up with some big-time saves. However, the game almost ended when a puck went off Bernie Nicholls' skate.

JOHN DELLAPINA: "I think you feared it a little bit because it's confirmation bias. Those are the things you remember and people always talk about it, but it's usually going to be a dirty goal or deflection. In a perfect world, Leetch or Messier or Nicholls would have scored. You want it to be a perfect shot. But ultimately it was a beautiful picture the way it ended. To this day I don't know how Howie Rose got that call right, but I guess he had the unbelievably perfect line, because I was 20 feet from it and I didn't know it was Matteau. It wasn't clear to me who put the puck in the net.

"I saw Matteau wrap it around but I couldn't tell immediately if he was the one who put it in the net. I'm sure Marty would like to have the goal back, but you know, what doesn't kill you makes you stronger. As John (Giannone) and I recall, we knew what we were watching was epic and that is the moment; it's right in front of us. There's a picture hanging in the Rangers practice facility and you can see me standing up and pointing. And I do get some grief for it, but I was not cheering.

"Walking into that Devils' locker room was a tough thing afterward. I mean it was devastation, but it really was a lot of class. I know guys like Ken Daneyko, who had a personal relationship with Mark Messier, made a point to congratulate Messier. I know John McMullen walked from one end to The Garden to the other to congratulate the Rangers owners. And it took a lot to do that. Bernie Nicholls, who was a guy who was largely happy go lucky, I saw him on the bus just crying for an hour after the game. For him it might've been his only shot to win the Stanley Cup. Right. When I remember that night I remember the Rangers' triumph, but I also remember it as devastating for the Devils."

MOST UNFORGETTABLE RANGERS MOMENT

JOHN GIANNONE: "I would think anybody's whose been around the Rangers or is a Rangers fan would have to list their signature moment in our lifetimes as the moment that Gary Bettman handed the Stanley Cup to Mark Messier. I think back to that moment and to everything that's happened since and unfortunately, when Gary Bettman takes the ice he's usually met with a chorus of boos. But I don't remember that happening that night.

"There was such euphoria inside The Garden that this team had finally won the Stanley Cup that it didn't matter who was going to hand off the Stanley Cup to Mark Messier. Just the look on his face and just his mouth wide open, he had done this four or five times before, and yet, for him, it was a completely different, almost first time win because of his understanding of what it meant to New York. I remember being in the building working for The Daily News at the time and watching the progression of who gets The Cup, who gives it to whom and what if anything do they say to each other. And I remember, Mike Richter handed it to Nick Kypreos and he just said one word, 'finally!' That's the only thing he said.

"Most of the time these days, players might throw a curse word out there because it just sort of represents how much blood sweat and tears goes into winning that trophy and the mental toil of getting it. But, remembering the noise in the building and some of the songs that were playing on the loudspeaker, like, Heroes, When A Hero Comes Along was playing and watching the confetti fall from The Garden roof. Just remembering the looks on every single player's face. And remembering that the first time a Russian had ever lifted the Stanley Cup over his head and it was Alexei Kovalev.

"And remember, hearing throughout, ever since Fetisov become the first Russian to play in the NHL, 'oh those guys are cut from a different cloth. They're so much more mechanical and so much more robotic. They don't bring the same emotion level as North American players. And then to watch Kovalev, and to watch the four Russians on that team -- Kovalev, (Sergei) Zubov, (Sergei) Nemchinov, and (Alexander) Karpovtsev -- just rejoice in winning the Stanley Cup. You got the feeling it was probably going to be the greatest snapshot you were ever going to get from this franchise. And to this day it still is.

"Back in those days they didn't do that (bring the reporters on to the ice). I was in the portal box above the Zamboni entrance; right in the corner and to the left of where the visiting goaltender was, which was Kirk McLean during that series. My view was basically from that left corner, Eighth Avenue end, staring straight down the middle at the Stanley Cup.

"Watching it being walked out by the gentlemen, who to this day are still the keepers of The Cup, walking out in white gloves and treating it with the reverence it deserves and putting it on the pedestal and having Gary Bettman come out and say, 'New York, after 54-years your long wait is over! Mark Messier, come get the Stanley Cup!' I still remember those words to this day. And then, the look on Messier's face, he took The Cup and he immediately made a gesture with his head because his hands were filled, as if to tell his team, 'get over here, get over here.'

"Then, one-by-one, they just started passing it to each other. And I remember just standing there chronicling who gave it to whom, and that was one of our stories in the Daily News the next day; how The Cup was passed around The Garden for the first time in 54-years."

6 ALLAN KREDA (NY TIMES) GAME 6: 2014 EASTERN CONFERENCE SECOND-ROUND (@MSG) MAY 11, 2014 NYR 3, PIT 1

BACKGROUND

New York City, specifically the borough of Brooklyn, is known for its deep love of sports. If you think about it, you can probably name dozens upon dozens of professional athletes, broadcasters and journalists alike, who trace their roots back to Brooklyn.

Just off the top of my head you have names like: Joe Torre, Stan Fischler, Carmelo Anthony, Phil Rizzuto and Sandy Koufax; the list goes on and on. And don't forget about ace NY Times reporter, Allan Kreda.

While many fans know Allan Kreda as the man who has covered the NY Rangers and NY Islanders for over a decade, they don't usually know that he almost didn't become a sports writer.

In fact, when Kreda was a student at CUNY Brooklyn College he wasn't even a journalism major. But that soon changed thanks to a single news writing class taught by Professor Bruce Porter.

"Porter, who was the leader of the journalism program at that time, took a liking to me and my writing," said Kreda. "And he suggested that for the next semester I should get an internship to obtain some experience in the field."

So, at the urging of Professor Porter, Kreda applied for and was granted an internship with a well known alumni of Brooklyn College, "The Hockey Maven," Stan Fischler.

"That was in 1985," Kreda explains. "And it's still going strong today. After many forms of my writing and going from The Associated Press to Bloomberg News to The New York Times currently and a host of magazines and other outlets in between, I've essentially been around the Rangers in one form or another for 30 years."

With his wealth of experience guiding him, Allan Kreda has been a key witness to many memorable Rangers moments. But one stands out above the rest. And it's partially to do with his close relationship to the player involved.

The game? Try Game 6 of the 2014 Eastern Conference Second-Round matchup between the Rangers and the Pittsburgh Penguins. The player? Newly minted Hockey Hall of Famer, Martin St. Louis.

MOST UNFORGETTABLE RANGERS GAME

By now, most of you know the story. The New York Rangers entered the 2013-14 season in a state of uncertainty and high expectations. That's what happens when a team in "win-now mode" fires its' Head Coach after failing to take the necessary "next steps."

So, after falling to the Bruins in the second-round of the 2012-13 playoffs, the Blueshirts bid *Au revoir* to Head Coach John Tortorella, and said *Bonjour* to the mild-mannered, Alain Vigneault, who ironically enough, had just been fired by the Vancouver Canucks for failing to guide his veteran-laden team to a Stanley Cup Championship. Perhaps he'd have better luck in New York?

The season started out inauspiciously, as the Blueshirts dropped seven of their first 10 games to put them in an early hole in the standings. But they quickly righted the ship with seven wins in their next nine games.

From there, the New York sextet began to show the rest of the league that they were a different team from years past. Gone were the days of the Rangers having to win every game 2-1, or 1-0. These Blueshirts could score. Gone was Tortorella's "Black and Blueshirts" system. In its' place, Vigneault installed an up-tempo, fast break offense that had the Rangers storming up the standings.

By the time the regular season came to a close, New York had accumulated 96 points, their second-highest points total since the 2007-08 campaign. And with those 96 points came a second-place finish in the new Metropolitan Division.

Thanks to the NHL's realignment, and implementation of a new playoff system, the Rangers were set to host the third-place Flyers in the opening round of the Stanley Cup playoffs.

A back-and-forth series ensued as the Blueshirts had trouble adjusting to the Flyers' brutal style of play. But a Game 3 win, buoyed by the insertion of Daniel Carcillo into the lineup, put New York up 2-1 in the series. And they eventually closed out the series victory with a Game 7 win over the Flyers at Madison Square Garden.

Next it was on to Pittsburgh to face the first-place Penguins.

The series started off well for the Rangers, as they "scored two goals" in overtime to take Game 1 by the score of 3-2. Unfortunately, that's when things turned ugly. Incensed that the Blueshirts had beaten them in their own building in Game 1, the Penguins came out flying in Game 2; coasting to a 3-0 victory as the series shifted to New York.

Games 3 and 4 were more of the same as the Penguins roasted the Rangers by a combined score of 6-2; putting the Blueshirts one loss away from being eliminated.

"I remember thinking, after they lost Game 4, that the series was over," recalled Kreda. "Pittsburgh was dominating them. I believe Marc-Andre Fleury had a shutout in Game 3. The Rangers looked completely done. It seemed like going back to Pittsburgh was a formality, and then we saw the terrible news the night before Game 5."

That "terrible news" was the tragic passing of Martin St. Louis' Mother, France.

ALLAN KREDA: "It was literally 8pm or 9pm the night before when we saw that news and wondered, wow, what is this? How could he possibly play? It was very difficult news for anyone at anytime, let alone in the middle of the playoffs. The Islanders had gone through something similar in 1984 when Denis Potvin's dad passed away during their Cup run; late in their Cup run. He had to play with a heavy heart and he talks about it to this day, how impactful it was, how exhausting it was and how difficult it was.

"I can only imagine what it was like for Marty, who was very close to his mom. It happened suddenly and they were still in the middle of the series. It seemed like the team basically decided to play for him, be there for him and somehow carry on for him. So they went into Pittsburgh and won Game 5; dominating 5-1. They really reversed any momentum the Penguins had generated by winning the two games at The Garden, after splitting the first two games in Pittsburgh.

"So, now you have this dynamic of the Rangers having won a game on the road, coming home and playing on Mother's Day of all days. You just could feel the buildup and knowing how good that Rangers team was in big games. It seemed like they were suddenly in the driver's seat; down 3-2. It looked like, felt like that's what was happening, especially the way they played in Game 5; overwhelming the Penguins the way they did.

"I remember coach Alain Vigneault, before the game, we asked him about his thoughts and feelings going into that afternoon's game. He just said, 'you know, it's Mother's Day. We expect the emotions to run high. None of us would be shocked by anything we're about to see here.' He was cognizant of Marty's delicate emotions, as any of us would be.

"I really sensed that the team, the crowd, even the city if you can stretch it to that length, was behind him. The story had been told. The Rangers take over the airwaves when they are in the playoffs and they're winning. And this team seemed to be among their better teams. They had beaten the Flyers in the first-round; it took seven games, but they had Henrik at his best and they were rolling. Pittsburgh wasn't easy to beat, but with this kind of momentum shift, it felt like Game 6 was going to be a special one.

"France St. Louis had had a heart attack, it was pretty instantaneous. She was 63-years-old and very close to Marty. She had been someone who had always told him he could overcome the odds. Knowing Marty as I do, I'm not surprised how he was built and how he made himself so great through sheer determination. Usually a parent can help you with that in a very big way. And apparently France St Louis was that power behind him.

"The Garden was very loud as the game was getting set to start. Of course, the anthem with the playoffs, Rangers games are always big. The buildup was nothing less than you'd expect. There were balloons and all the noise they could muster. I'm sure Marty was on the ice for starting lineups too. It was a deafening roar. I believe John Amirante sang the anthem that day. It was just the biggest, loudest ovation you could have.

"I don't remember the Rangers ever playing a game, a home game on Mother's Day before, let alone a game on Mother's Day with this backdrop; this backstory. It felt like something with Marty would happen before it even happened.

"I just remember the puck in that corner, down there to the left of where the Zamboni entrance is. I'm pretty sure Marty started that game on the ice and then he was back on a little over three minutes later when the puck found him.

"It was kind of a jumble in front of the net. I know Derek Stepan was in there and it wound up on Marty's stick. He was basically to Marc-Andre Fleury's left, looking out from the goal, and before you could blink again the puck was in the net and Marty was overwhelmed by his teammates as they swarmed in the corner. He scored the first goal and the place went berserk.

"I think we all had Goosebumps from that; how could you not? It was emotional for every single person in that crowd, on the ice and in the press box to see him score the goal. If we had taken a poll at that moment, we all probably would have been 99 percent sure the Rangers were going to win the game; how could they not?

"And they kept the pressure on throughout; Carl Hagelin scored 6:25 in. The Penguins did manage to get one back late in the first, thanks to Brandon Sutter. But when the Rangers had a lead in the playoffs, with Henrik Lundqvist at his best, that's all they needed. They kept rolling. Marty didn't score again, but he didn't have to. He did everything he needed to do to lift the team and probably himself. It was very difficult and emotionally charged for him. I know his dad was in the crowd, as was his sister, his family, his kids and his wife. It was a major emotional wave for everybody.

"Then the Rangers just kept the clamps on, just like a typical game for the 2014 and 2015 teams. They just smothered the Penguins and didn't really let them do anything. They basically played 25 minutes with a two-goal lead and it probably didn't matter. The Penguins still mustered 37 shots on Henrik Lundqvist. But it didn't matter. It was a game they weren't going to lose for Marty. I think the only thing I really remember from that game is that goal. It stands alone in Rangers' lore.

"I'm sure if you asked Marty, he would say it's got to be right up there with winning The Cup and his other illustrious career highlights.

"I remember a very emotional sort of exhausted feeling from the team, even knowing they had to go back to Pittsburgh for Game 7. They had wrestled away the momentum. They had it now and they were playing on all cylinders. Suddenly, for a team that was done by all indications, physically, emotionally, in every other way, to now have a chance to win the series as the Penguins did back home; the sense was the Rangers had to be the favorites after Game 6.

"After the game, coach Vigneault marveled at Marty's ability to raise his game. His teammates, I'm sure, had a bunch of tears themselves. They were very close to Marty. I'm sure they shared some tears on the bench and in the room. And I'm pretty sure Marty got the game hat that day as well. When everyone was leaving the building, they were feeling like they had just seen something very special and that the Rangers would be back; this wasn't the last time they'd see them that season."

COMMENTARY FROM OTHERS AT THE GAME

AL TRAUTWIG: "What I remember is you can't make this stuff up. It's beyond sports and it's why I love sports. When something like that happens, it's Mother's Day and he's (Marty St. Louis) lost his mom. They win the game and he's part of it. It's like a fairy tale. It's crazy. And to me being on the air for moments like that is what I live for. I mean, I live for coming up with the phrase or sentence or paragraph to put that in perspective for what it was. And I remember that being really challenging, but it was just so easy. You know you just can't make it up."

LARRY BROOKS: "She (France St. Louis) had died on the night before Game 5. I remember we were out in Pittsburgh and the news came across and we were just wondering if he was going to play or not. He and Nash had been awful in Game 4, and in fact, I think I grabbed them both after the game and I'm pretty sure Marty said it was the worst game he'd ever played in his career; they were booed off the ice. The Rangers were booed off the ice after Game 4.

"And clearly, his mom's death was the catalyst in their turnaround. There's no question about it. They played on such an almost supernatural emotion. They dominated Game 5, but it was all emotion. You could just see it was all raw emotion. They came back for Game 6 here (at The Garden) and it was as loud as the building probably had been in a couple of years.

"They had just gone through the make over. I think it was the first full year of the bridges here at The Garden. The entire architecture had been changed; it's a quiet building now in New York. I think the architects had something to do with it. And I think the prices have something to do with it. But even in the playoffs, the building is one of the more quiet buildings in the league.

"I had actually written about it for that day, and that night it was loud. It almost reminded you of the old days where it was just so noisy here and the building was intimidating. But again, it was a night of emotion. He (Marty St. Louis) scored in front; I think the puck deflected off of him. And I don't think there was any doubt they were going to win that game.

"I mean, I don't think there was any doubt. The question was whether they're going to be able to win Game 7. And (Henrik) Lundqvist played one of the great games of his career and they won Game 7 2-1. It was a series they won purely on emotion. They would have lost in five I think. And then who knows what would have happened if they had gone out meekly in five games that year. But they didn't."

MOST UNFORGETTABLE RANGERS MOMENT

ALLAN KREDA: "Well, I mean, The Cup, of course, stands alone. But in a different generational moment, there have been a lot. But since we're talking about 2014 and the run to The Final and just how rarely that happens. The Rangers have only been to The Final four times in my lifetime: 1972, when I was not even seven yet; 1979, when I was in Junior High School. That was epic, but I wasn't here for those games so I can't count that, but I watched them all. 1979 was unique because, beating the Islanders when they were at the top of their absolute game before they won The Cups, still is as good as it gets for Rangers fans of a certain generation. It was a special run in '79. 1994 speaks for itself; of course.

"2014 had its' moments. And aside from the one we just talked about, I would say Dominic Moore's goal in Game 6; the game-winning goal in a 1-0 game. Game 6 against Montreal put the Rangers into The Final. It was as loud as the building has ever been; probably in all the times I've been here and it goes back a long way, even with the acoustical changes in this new Garden. The Rangers getting a chance at The Final, which we only get to see every 20 years if we're lucky; that would be right up there."

7 DON LA GRECA (ESPN RADIO)
GAME 1: 2014 EASTERN CONFERENCE SECOND ROUND (@CONSOL ENERGY CENTER) MAY 2, 2014 NYR 3, PIT 2 (OT)

BACKGROUND

If you are an avid listener of sports talk radio shows, there's a very good chance you've heard of Don La Greca. From being a co-host on The Michael Kay Show, with Michael Kay, to broadcasting Rangers games with the likes of Kenny Albert and Dave Maloney, La Greca has made quite the name for himself among sports fans.

But how did this New Jersey native become the mainstream radio voice he is today?

"I won a communications award my senior year of High School," said La Greca. "And it gave me the idea that I should try communications in college. I was always interested, but I was trying out to be a college baseball player. But I got cut and I walked into the radio station at Ramapo College and I thought, 'well, I'm not going to be a baseball player, so I may as well try the communications route.' They had a radio station on campus and I figured, 'well, if I can't play it, I'll cover it.' So I did the baseball and basketball games for Ramapo's radio station.

"Then, from college, I interned at K-Rock, which was the classic rock station in New York in 1990. That's where I met Maria Milito, a DJ at K-Rock, whose husband, Pete Walker, worked at Sports Phone. And I got the job at Sports Phone, the 976131 number, to get scores. A lot of people started there, including; Howie Rose, Al Trautwig, Bob Papa,

Michael Kay and I did updates there from 1992-2000. But in the middle of working there, I got an opportunity to meet a guy named Andy Roth, who knew Steve Malzberg, who got me a part-time gig at 1010 WINS.

"From 1010 WINS, Mark Chernoff heard me on The Fan and I started doing updates on The Fan. And then, when ESPN Radio started, Steve Malzberg, who was the one who got me the gig at 1010 Wins, was doing the hiring at ESPN and he recommended me, so I started working at ESPN and the rest is history.

"I kind of had a crazy way of getting from Point A to Point B."

After moving around a bit early in his career, La Greca has since found a steady home at ESPN Radio, where he also does the NY Rangers' radio broadcasts with Kenny Albert and Dave Maloney.

And in true Don La Greca fashion, the same way he had a "crazy way of getting from Point A to Point B," he also got the chance to call a rather "crazy" Rangers' playoff game.

Now, if you are a hockey fan, you know that overtime hockey is played under sudden-death rules, meaning the first team to score a goal wins. In other words, it's impossible to score more than one goal in a single overtime period. Or is it?

Well, as it turns out, Don La Greca's most memorable Rangers' game involves the rarest instance in which not one, but two goals were "scored" in the same overtime period. It just so happens that this oddity occurred during Game 1 of the 2014 Eastern Conference Semi-Final matchup between the New York Rangers and the Pittsburgh Penguins.

MOST UNFORGETTABLE RANGERS GAME

The 2013-14 season was a fruitful one for the Rangers, as they thrived under the guidance of new Head Coach, Alain Vigneault.

In fact, they thrived so much that they were seen as serious Stanley Cup contenders when the playoffs began.

However, the opening round was anything but easy for New York as they ran into a game Philadelphia Flyers team who just didn't know how to give up. But when it was all said and done, the Rangers managed to secure the four wins necessary to send the Flyers home for the summer and cash their own ticket to the second-round of the playoffs, where an old rival was waiting.

Dating back to the early-1990s the Rangers and Penguins engaged in a heated rivalry throughout both the regular seasons and the playoffs. Who could ever forget Adam Graves breaking Mario Lemieux's hand during the 1992 Patrick Division Final?

Now, roughly two decades later, the Rangers and Penguins were once again at each other's throats, as they battled for the right to advance to the Eastern Conference Final; only this time, you had Henrik Lundqvist, Derick Brassard and Benoit Pouliot for the Rangers facing off against Sidney Crosby, Evgeni Malkin and Marc-Andre Fleury for the Penguins.

Game 1 of the series was played in Pittsburgh and, as you might imagine, it was a hard hitting, seesaw affair.

As is the case in any hockey game, but especially in the playoffs, it's crucial to score first. So, when Benoit Pouliot put the Rangers on the board 5:03 into the first period, things were looking good for New York. And things only got better near the end of the period when Brad Richards scored with under three minutes to go in the opening frame to put the visitors in the driver's seat -- up 2-0.

Unfortunately for the Blueshirts, Pittsburgh's superstar players weren't going to let the Rangers win the game without a fight. And in the middle of the second period, roughly six minutes apart, the Penguins scored two-goals to tie the game. The first came from Lee Stempniak and the second from James Neal.

With their two-goal lead a thing of the past; New York tried to regain control of the game, but to no avail. So the teams continued to battle for that elusive third goal and when the final horn sounded at the end of the third period, neither the Rangers nor the Penguins had added to their score sheet.

So as the saying goes, "Ladies and Gentlemen, please stand by for overtime."

And here's where I'll let Don La Greca pick up the story.

DON LA GRECA: "I had called playoff games before. And I had called some cool moments, but I'd never had an overtime game. So, I was in Pittsburgh doing the game and we're going to overtime and I'm nervous. I was like, 'geez this is crazy,' and there's no commercials. This is going to be a big moment, win or lose; it's going to be a call that could very easily be remembered.

"So I'm calling the game with Dave Maloney and in the overtime, Derick Brassard scored. But they waved the goal off, so they kept playing. And then, Benoit Pouliot put in the rebound and scored the game-winning goal.

"I called it as Brassard scoring the goal, but I followed the play and the official waved it off. Then, Pouliot scored and the replay showed that I had it right, Brassard had scored. It's kind of known as the 'Two-Goal Overtime;' you're not supposed to score twice in overtime.

"But I also remember that Dave had gotten so excited and you hear him yell when Brassard scored. And then the play continued. But what people don't know, is that Dave actually hit his hand on the parabolics. We were high-fiving each other and I was like; I can't believe that after growing up a Devils fan, I was celebrating an amazing Rangers' game against Pittsburgh.

"Just everything that went into that series, and it being my first overtime, the way they scored and for me to be on top of the call, it was just one of the craziest things I ever was involved in. And to be able to call it too and being on top of the action, it was really amazing.

"So, on that play, we're not exactly dead center at the new building in Pittsburgh, so that's the far side of the ice that I'm calling it from. And I remember Brassard comes in, takes a shot from the slot and when I'm calling the game; I usually go by the sound. Sometimes it's tough to tell if the puck goes in unless you're standing above it. Like, at The Garden sometimes, you can tell because you're right on top of the action.

"But in Pittsburgh, it's a big building and you're far away. So my little indicator is, did I hear a ping? The puck came out hard and I didn't hear the ping, so I say 'goal!' I said, 'he scores,' but I immediately see the official, who's to the right of the goal, wave it off -- immediately.

"So I was able to incorporate that into my call. Dave yells, so there's this feeling like they won the game, but they've got to continue to play. Some of the players were kind of half celebrating. The play was continuing but there was this surreal feeling of, is the game still going on? Is it not going on? Did anybody see? I saw the official wave it off. But sometimes a lot of people don't see that. The light never went on, but there's that indication of celebration and then the puck's loose to the right and Pouliot picks it up and it hammers home the rebound.

"So you know they won the game. It's either Brassard's goal is going to count or Pouliot's is going to count. But either way, you know they won the game. It was just that surreal feeling of, when did the game end and is there going to be some kind of like controversy, because there were some guys who stopped playing. But in my mind I knew the game was over. It was just a question of who scored the goal.

"So Dave and I are are analyzing it and I'm sticking to my guns saying I think Brassard scored the goal, but we weren't sure. And then they got the replay, but obviously replay didn't matter; it just determined who scored the goal. And usually what strikes me about that is that the goal is scored, game's over, everybody runs to the guy who scored the goal and he becomes a part of history.

"I mean how many guys score overtime goals in the playoffs? And especially in the second-round, especially against Pittsburgh and to not know who the heck scored the goal was just one of the more surreal moments that I remember about that series."

COMMENTARY FROM OTHERS AT THE GAME

LARRY BROOKS: "I just remember not being sure if the first one went in; was it (Derick) Brassard who scored or (Benoit) Pouliot who scored? They won that first game but then played so poorly in the next three that the first game didn't seem so memorable after they lost the next three the way they did. They were just terrible; just awful. They were awful in Game 4."

AL TRAUTWIG: "I think at that point, I still needed to find a way to believe the Rangers could win the series. And that was the moment that I realized they could win the series. I mean it's Sidney Crosby, it's the Penguins; it's a little bit uncharted territory. So, when they did that in that fashion, it made me really think that that was a wonderful series. And to me, as a fan -- which I normally am -- is a big deal."

MOST UNFORGETTABLE RANGERS MOMENT

DON LA GRECA: "It would be calling Game 1 of the Stanley Cup Final in 2014. Doc Emrick's brother-in-law or father-in-law had died and he couldn't call the game. So, Kenny (Albert) got taken off the game to fill in for Doc on television. And so I got the phone call to call Game 1. I was like, 'this is unbelievable! I'm going to call the Stanley Cup Final.' As I mentioned before, I got into hockey late, I didn't get into hockey until I was already 15, 16-years-old. Where as, with other sports, I was basically a fan from birth. But my passion for hockey was through the roof and I loved watching every playoff game and Stanley Cup Final.

"I remember driving around trying to find a signal for Penguins-North Stars in 1991. So here I am calling, a Stanley Cup Final game; I just didn't know where I was going, because the Blackhawks and Kings were playing in the Conference Final out west and they had gone seven. So, I was either going to go to Chicago or L.A. and I honestly wanted to go to Chicago for an Original Six matchup; I had never been to Chicago before. But the Kings won the game and the next thing I know, I'm flying out to the coast for Game 1 and Neil Best from Newsday is interviewing me about preparing for this opportunity to call Game 1. Going to the morning skate and just seeing all the media and just being a part of that was just unbelievably crazy.

"So I'm getting ready to call the game and it's the first time the Rangers are in the Stanley Cup in literally 20 years. I'm getting to call

Game 1 against the Kings and I really felt like the Rangers were going to win The Cup. Game 1 was a huge deal and the Rangers got off to a flying start; taking a 2-0 lead. They scored a couple of goals early. (Carl) Hagelin had a goal go off of a defenseman for the Kings. It went off of (Slava) Voynov and into the Kings' net.

"I remember the building being so loud and so electric and the NHL came in to videotape Dave (Maloney) and I doing the game, because if the Rangers won The Cup, they would show some of the calls. I felt like it was so perfect that it was in Hollywood, because I just felt like I was part of a movie. I got kind of thrown into this. I was just riding on adrenaline and I was on top of all the calls.

"For the Kings, (Kyle) Clifford scored late in the first period to make it 2-1 going into the second and then the Kings started to really dominate as they then tied the game. Then we went to the third period and the Rangers were hanging on. If you remember, they blew two, two-goal leads in the first two games of that series. The Kings were just bigger and more physical. You could see the Rangers begin to wear down.

"Then (Brian) Boyle took a penalty late in the third, so the Rangers have to kill a penalty that was going to spill into overtime and the action all of a sudden just opened up. Both teams had amazing opportunities and Hagelin had a breakaway that (Jonathan) Quick stopped late in the third period. Then the Kings came back and Dustin Brown had a great opportunity.

"(Anze) Kopitar came in on a two-on-one with (Jeff) Carter and there was about 30, 40 seconds of me just continually calling shot after shot after shot and then it went into overtime. I remember saying into my call, 'that we're going overtime and I need a break.' Dave then goes, 'what a great job by Don La Greca!' I literally collapsed in my seat. I'm on nerves and adrenaline. The play was back-and-forth and we went into overtime and I had survived.

"I was really hoping they'd score, it would be great moment. So we got into overtime, Dave and I are just sweating. I couldn't believe this was happening, because it's new for Dave too. The last time Dave was involved in a Stanley Cup Final was working for Fox. And then when he was with the Rangers was back when he went to The Final in 1979. So we're both going through this, we get into overtime and the Rangers killed the rest of the penalty. But again, it kept going the way it had gone for the last two periods, where the Kings were starting to really dominate. And then Dave says, 'this game is going to end on a turnover. You could just tell that this game is going to end on somebody turning the puck over.'

"So I'm watching out for that, because the scary thing about turnovers is, when you're doing play-by-play, you're on top of the action. But a turnover, everything can change. (Dan) Girardi had the puck between the circles, he's spent, he's at the end of a shift and he desperately throws the puck to the far boards to get it out of the zone. It was taken by; I believe it was Carter, who found Justin Williams. Now, if you know Justin Williams, he'd been a Rangers-killer forever, going back to his years with the Capitals. It just always seemed he was the guy -- I don't care what team he was on, Hurricanes, Capitals, Kings --who always seemed to kill the Rangers.

"The puck goes back to where Girardi was between the circles he fires the shot and he beats (Henrik) Lundqvist. Now, I'm on top of the call and it got played a lot. Going back and listening to it, the crowd was so loud you almost don't hear my call. Like you hear me say, 'Justin Williams,' but then the crowd just went nuts.

"I was proud to be on top of the call, because you don't want to screw up an overtime playoff game. But, it was like that disappointment of, it started out 2-0 and you figure you're on your way to a big Game 1 win. Then they blow the lead and to lose the way they did, I was just so drained afterwards. But it was easily the greatest thing that's happened to me in my career. To be able to call a Stanley Cup Final, have it go to overtime and to be on top of the call, the fun that I had, it was just a surreal experience."

8 DAVE MALONEY (MSG NETWORKS)
2013-14 PLAYOFFS (@WELLS FARGO CENTER, @CONSOL ENERGY CENTER, @MSG)
APRIL 22, 2014; MAY 13, 2014; MAY 29, 2014
NYR 4, PHI 1; NYR 2, PIT 1; NYR 1, MTL 0

BACKGROUND

What you see is what you get when it comes to former-Rangers' captain, and current MSG Networks' analyst, Dave Maloney. He is as dignified today as he was when he served as the Rangers' captain from 1978 to 1981. In fact, he was, and is to this day, the youngest player to be named captain in Rangers' history.

There were reasonably high expectations on the lean defenseman from Kitchener, Ontario, when the Blueshirts opted to draft him in the first-round (14th overall) of the 1974 NHL Amateur Draft. And Maloney did not disappoint, compiling 295 points (70-G, 225-A) in 605 regular season games in New York.

Then, during the Rangers' 1980-81 playoff series against the Los Angeles Kings, Maloney got hurt and couldn't play, so he did the next best thing; he joined the broadcast booth.

"I had gotten hurt in the LA series of the 1980-81 playoffs and I ended up being the third guy in the radio booth with Marv Albert and Sal Messina," said Maloney. "We beat LA first, then beat St. Louis and then lost to the Islanders. So that started (my broadcasting experience)."

Maloney's first foray into the world of broadcasting peaked his interest and when he hung up his skates for good following the conclusion of the 1984-85 season -- he spent the second-half of that year playing for the Sabres -- he was intrigued by the possibility of going into broadcasting.

"I always had an interest and when I retired, I had an interest to pursue it," explained Maloney. "It wasn't going to be my full-time job; I was doing something else on a more professional basis." And that "more professional basis," turned out to be a job on Wall Street. Yet, the itch to be in the broadcast booth never went away.

"Whenever somebody needed somebody to fill-in, whether it was TV or radio, I usually got a call," Maloney recalled. "And I ended up doing some work for some Canadian networks. I had the NHL on FOX studio thing and I worked for the North Stars for a year. So I always kept my foot in the door and when the lockout came, I was afforded the opportunity to make a decision. And 13 years later, here I am."

Since joining MSG Networks full-time following the 2004-05 lockout, Maloney has done it all, in terms of broadcasting. "I started with the radio side, where I'm still quite involved, but my role has morphed to a little bit more television," explained Maloney. "I kind of do a lot of different things from that aspect and I like the fact that I'm the only one of the crew who does every game; either on the sidelines for TV or in the radio booth."

MOST UNFORGETTABLE RANGERS GAMES

During his time with MSG Networks, Dave Maloney has had the privilege of covering his fair share of exciting post-season runs. And arguably the most exciting was in 2014, when the Rangers made a run to the Stanley Cup Final for the first time since 1994.

Over the course of the 2013-14 playoffs, Maloney was a constant presence on the team's broadcasts, even as the national networks took over the play-calling responsibilities as the Rangers progressed through the rounds.

First up were the Philadelphia Flyers; a team Maloney despised going back to his playing days. "I hated playing Philly. I hated playing in Philly. I hated the Flyers' fans," exclaimed Maloney.

So, after the Rangers and Flyers split the opening two games at The Garden, the teams traveled to Philadelphia for the classic, "Swing Game," in Game 3.

DAVE MALONEY: "I remember Game 3, in Philadelphia, Danny Carcillo went into the lineup -- after the Flyers had had their way with us in Games 1 and 2, physically -- and basically said, 'that's enough.' I remember him, not *actually* flipping off the fans, but *basically* flipping off the Flyers' fans.

"Now, as the playoffs move along, you become a little more distanced from the team. So oftentimes we're not nearly as privy to what's going on with the heartbeat of the team in the playoffs." (Regional networks, like MSG Networks, don't hold the rights to their team's broadcasts in the post-season). "But that Flyers series probably hearkens back to my days of playing against the Flyers. In those days, that franchise probably had the least respect of mine, given the way they played.

"Given the way that series had set up, like I said, we split the first two. And I remember (Scott) Hartnell had had his way. (Wayne) Simmonds basically had his way in the first two games and to see one of our guys say, 'that's not going to happen anymore,' that was really cool."

Daniel Carcillo's third period goal essentially salted away the game as it gave the Rangers a commanding 4-1 lead with under 10 minutes to go in the game. And when the Blueshirts closed out the game by the same score, they took a 2-1 lead in the series. Of course, the Flyers still managed to push New York to a seventh game, which the Rangers won on home ice by the score of 2-1, but the tone for the series was set, thanks to Carcillo's actions throughout Game 3.

After disposing of the Flyers in the first-round, the Rangers moved onto another hated division rival, the Pittsburgh Penguins. And while the Blueshirts won Game 1 in overtime, it was the Penguins who controlled the series, as Pittsburgh went up three games to one after winning Games 2, 3 and 4.

Pittsburgh had a chance to close out the series on home ice in Game 5, but the Blueshirts, in support of teammate Martin St. Louis, stood tall and dominated the Penguins, en route to a 5-1 victory; momentarily staving off elimination.

You see, prior to Game 5, St. Louis, who had been acquired at the trade deadline from Tampa Bay as part of the package that sent Ryan Callahan to the Lightning, got the call that everybody dreads the most. His loving Mother, France St. Louis, had tragically passed away from a heart attack at age 63.

Distraught, St. Louis returned home to grieve with his Father, who promptly sent him back to the Rangers, telling his son that his Mother would have wanted him to play. So Marty returned to the team to play Game 5, during which he was held without a point. But his moment was soon at hand.

DAVE MALONEY: "We were down 3-1 going into Pittsburgh and, given the circumstances of Marty St. Louis' mother passing away, we had absolutely no business winning Game 5. But we did and convincingly so. It was one of those mystical things you certainly don't plan for. And it becomes a little bit like the Vegas story last year. They were galvanized by what happened at the hotel and in the parking lot. It becomes a bit of a banner and obviously it was beyond explaining or rationalizing.

"It was mystical that they could sit on the plane, having heard the news (about St. Louis' mother passing away) and then have to go out and play and to have it play out the way it did. They had no business having Game 5 play out the way it played out, given how they played in Game 4. I remember thinking about how it was a convincing win in Game 5, because it defied all logic. But I do remember thinking there must be a greater being out there, because on a logical sense they had no business winning the hockey game."

After living to fight another day, the Rangers and Penguins headed to New York for Game 6, which was to be played on Mother's Day. And who better to step-up for the Blueshirts than Martin St. Louis? 3:34 into the game, St. Louis scored what might be the most emotional goal of his career to give the Rangers an early 1-0 lead. From there, the Blueshirts continued what they started in Game 5, dominating the Penguins on their way to a 3-1 victory. And more importantly, their Game 6 victory brought them back from the brink to force a Game 7 back in Pittsburgh.

A Brian Boyle goal 5:25 into the game put New York on top in the winner-take-all affair and goalie Henrik Lundqvist was determined to carry his team past the Penguins. But an early second period goal by Jussi Jokinen knotted the score at one. That is, until Brad Richards restored the Rangers' lead moments later with a power-play goal.

With the Blueshirts now leading 2-1, Lundqvist put the team on his back and shutdown the mighty Penguins.

DAVE MALONEY: "In Game 7 the last 10 minutes had you on the edge of your seat. When you think about it, the team (the Rangers) was literally booed off the ice in Game 4. And now, here they were, in the last 10 minutes of Game 7 against the Penguins. You really were just kind of holding your breath. And Henrik was Henrik. And that's most games in memory. When you're on the edge of your seat in the booth, Henrik has been All World. And I've been very fortunate to be here while he's been the goaltender.

"I remember thinking that it was one shot either way. And the quality of chances Pittsburgh was throwing at the Rangers, it was absolute magic what Henrik was doing. I remember being on the edge of my seat because we never got out of our end. From that standpoint, I suppose having been an ex player, you get the sense of just how close the margin for error is, and you're at this point, and it's really one shot's going to make the difference.

"So you get caught up in the emotion, my hands were sweating, the palms of my hands were sweating and you're anxious; living play-to-play. I guess it's those moments in that game I remember; specifically given how everything had evolved in the series. The guy (Henrik Lundqvist) was just absolutely brilliant and we were living and dying with every save. Henrik was awesome."

Having completed their "mystical" comeback from a 3-1 series deficit, the Rangers were confident in their ability to secure victory in the Eastern Conference Final. But to do so, they must first get through a team who always gave them fits, the Montreal Canadiens. Going back to their inaugural season, the Blueshirts have traditionally struggled against the Canadiens; especially when the games were played in Montreal.

In fact, the Canadiens are the only team in NHL history that the Rangers have a sub-.400 points percentage against. (Think of points percentage as similar to win percentage in baseball). And given the fact that the Bruins were the only team the Rangers have faced more often over the years, you've got a recipe for disaster. Not to mention that Montreal employed arguably the best goalie in the game in the form of Carey Price.

But there were the Rangers, believing in themselves as they controlled Game 1 at the Bell Centre. And then something happened that really made fans believe the Rangers could get past Montreal; Carey Price got hurt.

The Canadiens' franchise goaltender suffered a gruesome leg injury when Chris Kreider "accidentally" ran over him in a goalmouth collision. Without their star netminder Montreal didn't have the same aura of invincibility about them. And while backup goaltender, Dustin Tokarski placed reasonably well throughout the series, his team did not. So, after four games, the Rangers held a 3-1 series lead and traveled to Montreal with a chance to close out the series in Game 5; looking to clinch their first appearance in the Stanley Cup Final since their Cup championship in 1993-94.

However, Montreal had no plans to be eliminated on home ice, winning Game 5 7-4 in convincing fashion. So the teams headed back to New York for Game 6, the Rangers still needing just one more victory to secure a trip to the Stanley Cup Final.

DAVE MALONEY: "It's funny, you almost have to pinch yourself to realize that you are that close to The Cup Final. Having played and having being privy to actually being part of the story, you do get a sense of what it's like to be in that situation and it's hard. It's hard not to be that way, but I want to be that way. I want to have that feeling of being intense, to be intensely involved and being emotionally attached; not so much physically.

"In Game 6 against Montreal it's the same sort of feeling. When I think about the games that really have gotten my heart going, they all have kind of the same thing. There's a drama to the story and there's a compete to the story. And the fine line between winning and losing is just that; it's that close."

The Rangers had no interest in going back to Montreal for a potential Game 7; they wanted to get it done on home ice, in front of their fans. And Dominic Moore did his best to make sure Game 6 ended with a Rangers' victory as he scored the only goal of the game, off a behind the net pass from Brian Boyle, with 18:07 gone by in the second period. From there it was in the hands of Henrik Lundqvist. And "The King" did not disappoint.

DAVE MALONEY: "Thomas Vanek had an opportunity to tie the game late, but Henrik was awesome; making that impossible save. I remember Vanek had not been much of a player in the series and I thought he was the most dangerous guy on the ice in Game 6. But Henrik made that save and now they were off to The Cup Final."

In all, Lundqvist needed to make 18 saves to lead the Rangers to victory in Game 6, and that's exactly what he did; delivering a shutout in front of the hometown fans and earning New York a spot in the Stanley Cup Final.

COMMENTARY FROM OTHERS AT THE GAMES

DEREK STEPAN (ON GAME 3 VS PHI): "Obviously it was a big point in the series. I think we had played really good hockey that season but towards the end of the year we kind of lost our Mojo a little bit. Going into that playoff series, I think we won Game 1 and Game 2 we really didn't play all that great. We were kind of just up and down with our consistency of play.

"We entered Carcillo into the lineup and it was a big game for him. He really brought a lot of energy for us and from that point on in the series we felt that we started to play better hockey. Carcillo really ignited the rivalry. I think he sparked both teams, but he really got our group going with really good energy."

STEPAN (ON PENGUINS SERIES): "It was a funny way that the series got to 3-1 so quickly. We felt that we played really good hockey and then, after Game 4 we were down 3-1. We were kind of feeling like, oh boy here we go. We're going to be done in five against a team who we feel we've played some pretty good hockey against. And we're going to leave this series earlier than we wanted to.

"Obviously what happened off the ice (St. Louis' mother passing away) is something that was never an easy thing and a guy like Marty was able to handle it like such a pro. As a group we just, we were still confident down 3-1.

"It almost kind of released us a little bit to say: 'we've got nothing to lose, let's go out and play. Look at one of our veteran leaders. He's coming to the rink ready to play hockey even with all the stuff that's going on in the background. I know that I had some conversations with him and he was just like, 'we're going to have her on our side up above us and we're going to come back and win this thing.' And that's exactly what we did.

"Me and Hags (Carl Hagelin) were on the ice with him (St. Louis, when he scored that goal on Mother's Day). It was something, a moment, I'll never forget in my career. Obviously the whole building knew what had gone on, but on the ice it was quiet. It was almost like a scene out of a movie. He scored, and me and Hags always talked about how the emotion was so strong with Marty that it was almost like it was super loud, but it was quiet in that moment and we were just all around Marty.

"It was a heavy moment for sure, but it was something that I'll never forget. And I know Hags and me talk about it a lot. Like this is just such a cool moment and it's something not many people get to be a part of."

Moving ahead to Game 7 against the Penguins, the Rangers were looking to complete their improbable comeback. And just like he has in the past, Henrik Lundqvist led the way. And Derek Stepan had arguably the best seat in the house for Lundqvist's heroics.

STEPAN: "I had a number of shifts during that time (the final 10 minutes of the game). Obviously, most of my time in New York, there have been multiple opportunities for me to talk about what Henrik Lundqvist did and how he kept us in games. And he was obviously a huge part, if not the biggest part of all of our deep runs, his goaltending was elite. And it was no different in that game. We leaned on him heavily and he answered the bell and stood strong for us."

STEPAN (ON MONTREAL SERIES): "No disrespect to the Montreal Canadiens, but we were coming off of a pretty good momentum swing with coming back from 3-1 down against a pretty good Pittsburgh team. We just felt that we had to keep playing the right way and if we did we were going to keep having good results. The momentum just carried over into Games 1 and 2. I felt like we played some really, really good hockey throughout the whole series. From our goaltender to our forward group, we were all playing and hitting on all cylinders.

"(As for Game 6) our leadership group and our coaching staff did a pretty good job of just saying, 'hey, it's another hockey game, let's just go play.' So I was kind of just on autopilot a little bit. I was in the Montreal-Rangers series. I wasn't looking past this game. My first couple of shifts I was just trying to handle the nerves as best I could. You just want to get into the swing of things and most of the time you can usually calm the nerves pretty good. That's all our focus was; this is just another hockey game. And we won the game in the fashion that, I think is perfect for us, because once again our best player was Henrik Lundqvist and we found a way to win 1-0.

"He was rock solid for us. I mean you see the highlights all the time (of his save on Thomas Vanek). It was a two-on-one and Vanek tried to make a pass across and it hit (Dan) Girardi's stick, popped up in the air and Hank made an athletic save to come up big. Obviously, if that goes into the net we might not even be talking about moving on past them. And once again, a guy who we keep talking about, he showed up big and shut the door so we could move on.

"We were all extremely happy and I think, if you ask most of the group, I think we kind of felt like we weren't done yet. We didn't feel like we'd done anything except for get to an opportunity to actually compete for The Cup. I thought we did a fairly good job of understanding that, hey this is great, but we've got another job to do. We had another seven-game series we wanted to try to get done."

PROUDEST RANGERS MOMENT

DAVE MALONEY: "I'm proud of the work I do and that Rangers fans, management and the team's coaching staff respect what I do. For me, I don't want to be a critic, after all my job is as an analyst, but I think you can analyze and say I'm describing what should've been done or shouldn't have been. I don't want any player to think I'm personally picking on them, because that's not my job. I guess what I'm most proud of, is when someone would say to me, 'we really like your honesty.'

"It's not so much that it's an honesty where I believe I'm right. It's not a right or wrong for me. It's just watching something evolve, explaining how it evolved and then going from there. I have worked with good people too. I mean I work with the best of the best in Donny (Don La Greca) and Kenny (Albert). And then, when I get to work with the TV crew, I'm with Sam (Rosen) and Joe (Micheletti). So, those are the things I think I'm most proud of."

9 JOE MICHELETTI (MSG NETWORKS)
GAME 6: 2012 EASTERN CONFERENCE QUARTER-FINALS
(@SCOTIABANK PLACE)
APRIL 23, 2012
NYR 3, OTT 2

BACKGROUND

The World works in mysterious ways. That sentiment has been true for millions of years and it will always be true; especially in the case of Joe Micheletti. As a steady defenseman in both the WHA and the NHL, Joe Micheletti enjoyed a six-year career in hockey. But when he hung up his skates following the 1981-82 season, the Hibbing, Minnesota native felt his future lay outside the world of professional hockey.

While most every Rangers fans alive today knows Micheletti as one-half of the Blueshirts' dynamic broadcasting duo, he initially had no interest in becoming a broadcaster.

"I never wanted to (become a broadcaster)," said Micheletti. "It was never a profession I even considered. I got into this business strictly by accident. When I finished playing in St. Louis I got into the investment business, with a company called EF Hutton. And that's what I was doing. I was selling stocks and bonds when Dan Kelly, who was one of the great all-time voices of hockey and was the play-by-play voice of St. Louis, called me up one day in late August and said he needed somebody to be his analyst on radio. And I didn't know Dan all that well. In fact, he had been a client of mine. About a year before, he asked me to buy him 500 shares of Anheuser-Busch and I said, 'great.' That's how our relationship began.

"But when he called me about being his analyst, he had never mentioned it before, he said, 'I need somebody and I think you could do it.' He said, 'we'll have fun and it'll get you back in the game; I'll help you. And it'll help your business to be back in the game, on the radio.'"

Just like that, Joe Micheletti was on the road to becoming one of the most respected broadcasters in the game. But it wasn't all smooth sailing for Joe.

"I showed up to a pre-season game in Peoria, Illinois," recalled Micheletti. "And it was the Blues versus Detroit. At the time, Peoria was where the Blues had their minor league team. And I just showed up there. We had Jack Buck, Dan Dierdorf, Bob Costas and Dan Kelly all working in St. Louis at the time, which made for some great national broadcasts.

"When you listen to them, you get spoiled because they make it sound so easy. So I showed up for the first game with Dan (Kelly) and I hadn't had an opportunity to talk about the business; so I showed up and didn't even have a pencil on me. I didn't know the first thing about what it took and how to prepare.

"Anyway, Dan almost fired me halfway through the first period because I interrupted him when he was calling a call, which is a bad thing to do. He told me he was going to fire me if I ever did that again."

Eventually, Micheletti settled into his new job and stayed there for two seasons, before becoming an Assistant Coach with the Blues. And after a few years doing that, he went back to the broadcast booth, this time calling games on television.

Gigs with the Minnesota North Stars and the Winter Olympics in Japan gave Joe some great experiences to hone his craft. And shortly after his stint doing the Winter Olympics, he received a call from MSG Networks asking if he would be willing to broadcast Islanders' game for them.

But Micheletti turned down MSG's offer because his buddy Eddie Westfall was currently employed in the position he was being offered. Meanwhile, later that summer (1999), Micheletti spoke with Westfall and Westfall told him that he wanted to take a step back from broadcasting because of all the "rigors of the constant travel."

Armed with this knowledge, and with Westfall's blessing, Micheletti eventually worked out a deal with MSG Networks to broadcast Islanders games. And when the 2004-05 NHL season was canceled due to a lockout, MSG Networks decided to shake things up a bit and Micheletti was placed on Rangers broadcasts starting with the 2005-06 campaign. And he's been there ever since, which means, he's been around for some truly fascinating Rangers games.

With Micheletti being around for so many memorable Rangers games and moments, you might be a little surprised to learn that the game which stands out to him the most is Game 6 of the 2012 Eastern Conference Quarter-Finals between the Blueshirts and the Senators.

MOST UNFORGETTABLE RANGERS GAME

The 2011-12 New York Rangers were a mix of heart, grit and superb goaltending. And they were also a bit of a surprise. But why were these Blueshirts such a surprise?

For one thing, they finished the regular season in first-place in the Atlantic Division with 109 points. That point total represented the highest in franchise history since their magical 1993-94 season.

And for another thing, the Rangers hadn't made it past the opening round of the playoffs since the 2007-08 campaign.

So, when the Blueshirts fell just a few points shy of winning the President's Trophy, it was quite the noteworthy surprise.

Led by franchise netminder, Henrik Lundqvist, the Rangers were notorious for being stingy when it came to giving up goals. In fact, Lundqvist was so sensational that year; he won the Vezina Trophy as the league's best goalie. But "The King" didn't do it alone. His teammates, both on offense and defense, were known for being card-carrying members of the "Black and Blueshirts" club; courtesy of the shot-blocking style of play favored by Head Coach, John Tortorella.

The one thing the New York sextet did lack, was offensive production. It seemed like every game was decided by a single goal. And often times it was.

Nevertheless, the Rangers were a team on a mission when the playoffs began. And their first-round matchup against the Ottawa Senators proved just how phenomenal Henrik Lundqvist really was; and how scarce their scoring was. In the seven-game series, which the Blueshirts ultimately won, they only mustered 14 goals; that's an average of just two goals per game.

But I'm getting ahead of myself.

The Rangers and Senators traded victories through the first four games of the series; three of which were decided by a lone goal. And that set-up a very important Game 5 at Madison Square Garden, where the winner would go up 3-2 in the series and have two chances to close out their opponent. Unfortunately for New York, Ottawa won the game 2-0 behind a masterful 41-save shutout from Craig Anderson. And two Jason Spezza goals provided the only scoring.

So there they were, the Rangers were staring elimination in the face, on the verge of another too soon playoff exit. Their goal was clear, win Game 6 in Ottawa and come back home to win Game 7.

Here's Joe Micheletti's take on that fateful Game 6 in Ottawa.

JOE MICHELETTI: "As far as I'm concerned, the best games, the best performances, the best stories and the best storylines all happen in the playoffs. So, as good as so many of the regular season games are, to me the playoffs are the best. And that 2012 first-round matchup between Ottawa and the Rangers was a tremendous series.

"Lundqvist was great. Craig Anderson was in goal for Ottawa and he almost never loses at MSG. It was a heck of a series. It was so tough and so close. It was a series where, if I remember correctly, Chris Neil hit Brian Boyle just inside the blue line while cutting across the ice. It was a nasty, tough series.

"Then, Ottawa wound up winning Game 5 at MSG to take a 3-2 series lead. So, here were the Rangers, down 3-2 and the momentum was on Ottawa's side. Their goaltender was playing great and they were a really physical team. You just knew, going up to Ottawa, something special had to happen in order for the Rangers to win the game. It was just such a close series; I believe there was maybe a one-goal difference between the two teams. That's really how close it was and the Rangers didn't have any momentum heading into Game 6.

"Ottawa was the home team, and they obviously had a very good team. The city of Ottawa was fired up. There was a buzz in the building that you only get in the playoffs. And then, the Rangers' Brandon Prust came out in the first period and just set the tone for the game.

"Prust didn't set the tone offensively, even though Brandon was a better player than people give him credit for. Rather, he set the tone for the Rangers physically. And that gave them back the momentum in the first period. The playoffs are about an unexpected person doing something to turn the tide or help you, or help your team win. Brandon didn't do it by scoring a couple of goals. He did it by coming out and changing the momentum of the series and changing the mindset of both teams.

"I'll never forget, in the first period, he challenged and fought Chris Neil. And he did it all without putting his team shorthanded. He just changed the game. And the Rangers went on to win 3-2 to tie the series and come back to New York for Game 7.

"That game just stands out in my mind because, I don't think dire straights is the perfect phrase to use, but the momentum was going the other way. And the Rangers were going into a hostile environment. It was just Prust who started it and then you could see his teammates kind of follow his lead and away they went; they found a way to get going and they found a way to win.

"It was such a great series and you knew you weren't going to get a soft goal, because Lundqvist and Andersson weren't going to give that up. But you had to try and find a way to take the crowd out of it. And that's what the Rangers were able to come out and do.

"Coach John Tortorella had them fired up and ready to go play. And he didn't need to say much because it was the playoffs and players get up for that. And Brandon wasn't the biggest guy, but he had a heart of gold. Then everybody else followed and that's what it took. And boy, Oh boy, you could feel it. You just had this feeling as we were doing the game, especially in that first period, that okay they've got something here. They got a little bit of an edge, more of an edge than Ottawa had. And that's when they regained their momentum."

COMMENTARY FROM OTHERS AT THE GAME

LARRY BROOKS: "Well, what I remember about Game 6 was (Brandon) Prust fighting Chris Neil, taking on Chris Neil. Neil had concussed (Brian) Boyle, who had had a great round and was actually their best player; which tells you how the Rangers played in the first four or five games of that series. They had a tough time getting going. It was a mean, physical series. Ottawa played very, very well and Neil had been kind of bullying the Rangers. And Brandon Prust took him on in the first period of Game 6. I don't think he did all that well in the fight, but it didn't matter.

"I think the Rangers scored two or three goals in a really short time in the second period and kind of took over the game. I remember thinking that the entire season was going to be a waste if they had lost Game 6 in Ottawa. It was their first real test of the year. They had gone into first place in December that year and they were great. They played great.

"They got momentum rolling in December and they never stopped honestly. And so they had never really had this. They'd never really had a game where they were tested. They had just rolled through the second half of the year. They had a chance actually to win the President's Trophy and I think they lost their last two and maybe three of the last four.

"But it wasn't really a paramount objective of theirs to win it. They didn't play great the last week or so down the stretch, last couple of weeks I don't think. And they won the game in Ottawa, which was a real test of their resolve. And then they won Game 7 2-1; which it seems like they won every Game 7 they played 2-1 for two or three years.

"But Game 6 was a big-time game for them. It was a big-time series. (Carl) Hagelin was suspended for elbowing (Daniel) Alfredsson. There was the Neil hit on Boyle, which didn't receive any supplementary discipline. One of their guys -- (Milan) Michalek -- I think kicked Dan (Girardi) in a goalmouth scramble late in Game 6 when the Rangers were up by a goal. So it was a real nasty series; good series."

MOST THANKFUL RANGERS MOMENT

JOE MICHELETTI: "Well, you see, that's a difficult question for me to answer because that's not the way I broadcast (games); never has been, never will be. And I don't criticize anybody else who has a certain moniker that they use, that when you hear it, you go, 'oh that's such and such who uses that during a game.' I've never done it; it's probably the way I learned.

"I can't come up with something that I said that (was so memorable). I always think this, and I've thought this from the day I got into broadcasting; what we do is no different than what a sports team, a hockey team does. For us to be good, that's the way I look at it, yes, you would certainly want your team to win, but our job is to not miss anything during a game. And to be able to do that, you need your producer, your director, (and others). Chris Ebert is our Producer. Larry Roth is our Director. Steve Napolitani is our Associate Director. Brian Gallagher does all of our graphics.

"Then you need great cameramen and you need people who listen. And you need people who find you things you don't see. So, at the end of it, if I say something on the air, like if I say, 'I think that was deflected. It looked to me like it deflected off a skate,' that's the way it looks to me. So, if I see it that way and I say it that way, there's always a chance I'm going to be wrong. But now, you have all these great people who find it. And that's not easy to do because you have to have people who understand the game.

"I've been really fortunate that I've had the chance to work with all these people who help me look good. And I've had this conversation with many people. This is a team. Everybody in the truck, Sam (Rosen) and whoever else I work with, expects me to be prepared for the game and to do my job. And that's to analyze and tell people why things are going on; just as they have a responsibility to me and to everybody else on the crew to do their job as best they can.

"If you have good people and their hearts are in the right place and everybody's thinking the same thing about how this game has to be better than our last game, that's when you have a great broadcast. That's not something you can bring to the booth. You prepare, but so many things can and do happen during the course of the game that the best thing for us is when you never have to look at your notes; because the game is dictating what you say and what you see. That's the thing I'm so fortunate about. So, I've never had a moniker of any kind and I've never wanted one, because you have to say things that fit your personality and that's not my personality.

"I started in this business with Dan Kelly, who's as good as it gets, on radio, and he taught me to be professional. He taught me to be fair and he showed me how to work and what I needed to do at this job. We never did anything gimmicky. And not everything is gimmicky. I never had a gimmick, it just wasn't my personality. I'm just watching the game and if I see something I just try to explain what I see. Again, I don't mock some of them who are great who you hear around the league or in different sports. I just don't have one."

10 PAT O'KEEFE (NEWS 12)
GAME 6: 2014 EASTERN CONFERENCE FINAL (@MSG)
MAY 29, 2014
NYR 1, MTL 0

BACKGROUND

"Kicked loose by Markov, he's shaken up on the play...McDonagh in the last eight...McDonagh able to play it back out... Subban there...The Rangers are going to The Final!"-- Doc Emrick, after the Rangers won Game 6 of the 2014 Eastern Conference Final to go back to the Stanley Cup Final for the first time in 20 years.

For every Rangers fan who wasn't alive or isn't old enough to remember 1994, Doc Emrick's call at the end of Game 6 of the 2014 Eastern Conference Final against Montreal represents a feeling of jubilant release 20 years in the making. And just like in 1994, if you were watching the game in 2014, you will always remember where you were when the Rangers punched their ticket to the Stanley Cup Final.

And while The Garden was a packed house on the night of May 29, 2014, one man had a view better than all but a few of the 18,000-plus people inside the building. And that man was Pat O'Keefe, a young reporter for News 12.

Many of you might be wondering how Pat came to be a reporter on that night, well here's how.

"It's (being a sports reporter) always what I wanted to do," said O'Keefe. "When I was growing up I was into sports and not much else. I always knew that I wanted to work in sports in some capacity, whether that was as a sports writer, broadcaster, TV anchor or as a play-by-play announcer; I just wanted to work in sports. And as it has turned out, I've actually been lucky enough to work in sports in all of those areas.

"My first job in broadcasting was as a play-by-play announcer for Rocky Mountain College in Billings, Montana. You see, I graduated college in 2003 -- from SUNY Brockport -- and I moved out to Montana that September to do play-by-play for the basketball teams there. It was a seven-month commitment and I was going to be done by March.

"My plan was to get some experience and see what was next. So, while I was out there I was able to secure a job as the Morning Drive Time Host on the news talk radio station in Billings. And I didn't leave there for close to two years. From Billings I moved to Anchorage, Alaska, where I got my first full-time TV job as the Sports Director for the ABC affiliate in Alaska. I worked there for 18 months, at which point, in January of 2007, I decided I had been away from New York for too long, so I decided to move home and see what I could find.

"Fortunately, two months after I moved home, I was hired by News 12 as a freelance Sports Anchor/Reporter. And I'll have been there 12 years come April 2019. So, during that time I've had the opportunity to cover the Rangers, the Knicks and everything else in New York sports, from the professional level all the way down to High School.

"And then of course, while I've been at News 12, I've been able to add to my resume by working with MSG Networks as a member of the Knicks and Rangers radio broadcast team. I'm in my fourth season there, doing most of the Knicks games and I probably do about a quarter of the Rangers games every year as the pre-game, intermission and post-game show host."

That's quite the impressive resume and it's a big part of the reason why Pat has been able to cover so many memorable Rangers games, including Game 6 of the 2014 Eastern Conference Final. So, now that you all know who Pat is, let's get back to his recollections from that exciting Spring night in 2014.

MOST UNFORGETTABLE RANGERS GAME

PAT O'KEEFE: "It was a fascinating, not only series, but playoff run, because you had the first two series which I believe they won in seven games each. Philadelphia went seven games and I remember it ended on a dramatic face-off with one second left. And then you had the Pittsburgh series. Pittsburgh was heavily favored. The Rangers fell behind three games to one and then Marty St. Louis' Mother passes away.

"He chose to stay with the team and play and the team rallied around him. He had the goal on Mother's Day and the Rangers come back and win that series and then you get to the Conference Final. And in the back of my mind I'm thinking, 'hey, this has been a great run. It's their second Conference Final in the last three years. Montreal is definitely the better team and has the best goalie in the NHL. Whatever happens, maybe they can make a series of it.'

"Then Game 1 they come out and they play really well. And of course you have the moment when Chris Kreider loses his balance on the ice and barrels into Carey Price, who ends up being lost for the series. So, the Rangers blow them out in Game 1 and then they also win Game 2. Now, all of a sudden you're like, 'Oh My God, this is the Rangers year.'

"I grew up in New York and in 1994 my mother's office had season tickets for the Rangers, so I went to those playoff games as a fan. And I grew up as a Rangers fan in New York City. Now I'm covering the team, but you still have that history of being able to relate and follow this team as a fan.

"So, in the back of your mind, now it's, you're up 2-0 and you're supposed to win the series, and that's not a comfortable position for Rangers fans. Then of course they come out, lose Game 3 at home and then Game 4 goes into overtime. You are a goal away from giving up this two game lead, and Montreal's not even playing their backup goaltender. They're actually playing their third-string guy, a kid named Dustin Tokarski. And he was playing out of his mind. Nobody had ever heard of him and I still have vivid memories of Doc Emrick yelling his name over and over throughout the series, because that's how well he played.

"And then, all of a sudden, St. Louis wins Game 4 and the series goes back to Montreal for Game 5. Now, for the Rangers, you're a game away from advancing to the Stanley Cup Final for the first time since 1994 and it's really the first time they'd gotten that close since 1997, when they went to the Conference Final. But they lost that series to the Flyers in five games. And other than that, the only other time they got to the Conference Final was in 2012 against New Jersey, when they lost in six games.

"Then they get blown out in Game 5, Hank gets pulled in the middle of the second period and the place is going crazy up there in Montreal. So they come back to New York for Game 6 and there was just so much nervous energy in the arena that night.

"I arrived at The Garden early that afternoon and I just remember, it took me forever to get the last three blocks from my garage. I'm there three, four hours before the game and there's just red, white and blue Rangers jerseys on the street. It was a beautiful Thursday evening; it was the last weekend in May. It was springtime and it's one of the best times of the year in New York.

"So I get into the arena a few hours before the game. Alain Vigneault did his pre-game talk and I had to do a report for News 12 The Bronx and News 12 Brooklyn. I had to do two separate reports, probably at like 5:20 and 5:50, just previewing the night. And the whole coverage was about just how nervous Rangers fans were. It wasn't a big sense of confidence coming off of the 7-4 loss in Game 5. It was more like; this is set up for us to fail.

"So, the first period goes by and I remember Tokarski was playing very well. But the Rangers had the better of the play. And yet, after 20 minutes when you're fully healthy and they're not, they're missing their best player, you're the ones who were supposed to win and they're the ones playing with house money and they have this hot goalie, because in the NHL, more than any other sport, you've seen this so many times before that one hot goalie can win a series for you. You started to get an uneasy feeling, because now we're 20 minutes into this game and the Rangers haven't broken through on this guy.

"Honestly, at that point, I was starting to look into making plans to go to Montreal for Game 7. I usually didn't travel with the team unless it was an elimination game and I was starting to look into what it would take to travel to Montreal to cover Game 7 of the Eastern Conference Final in two days time.

"Meanwhile, the moment I'll always remember, I was standing during the second period with a friend of mine who I went to high school with, named Andrew Bogusch, he works for CBS sports radio. I don't know who he was working for at the time, but he was covering the game for whatever radio station, it was either CBS or Sirius at the time. And like me he had grown up a Rangers fan. He grew up in Queens, we were a year apart in High School and we did the same thing.

"We have this good connection where we always see each other out at events like this and we hang out. So, we're standing there on the Chase Bridge and we're watching this play develop; I think it was late in the second period. And as far as the play goes, it was kind of a perfect play. The Rangers controlled the puck in the zone, Brian Boyle had it behind the net and he freed himself up to give himself a better angle. Dominic Moore came sliding down and Boyle was patient. He slid it right over to Moore, who, by the time he got the puck on his stick was only about a foot outside of the crease. I mean he was right there on top of Tokarski.

"What struck me was he didn't fire it right away. He waited half a second for something to open up in the goal. He found the opening, beating Tokarski and the place just absolutely exploded. As far as the play goes, it was funny, because the Rangers had such a hard time scoring that night, but that one goal came so easy to them.

"It was as if that was exactly how they would have drawn it up. And then of course it ended up being the only goal of the game, so nothing else came easy the rest of the night. I had mentioned how after Carey Price went down, the whole feeling around the series shifted because now Rangers fans were nervous because they were favored.

"Then, of course, you get to The Garden for Game 6 and it's shifted back the other way because there's a lot of nervous energy. You don't know if they're going to blow this thing or not. Well, after that goal went in, you got the sense the Rangers were not going to lose, because now you had a one-goal lead, it's almost the third period and you have Hank. You just figured Hank was not going to give up a goal in that situation. And neither were the Rangers, because they were the better team at that point in the series.

"As far as the third period goes, the biggest recollection I have was that's when they started to come up with a couple of chances. And that's when Hank had to step up and make a couple of saves down the stretch to keep it 1-0. I didn't have a great feel the Rangers were going to add to that. Tokarski was playing great, I think the Rangers outshot them like 2-to-1 in that game; I want to say it was like 34 to 17 or something like that. Lundqvist didn't have to do a lot the first two periods, but once Montreal emptied the tank, they came with the pressure and Lundqvist was able to stand up. And that ended up being the difference.

"That was classic Hank, I thought, because how many times in his career has he had to face 30, 35, 38 shots in a game and stand tall and maybe he gives up one too many goals. Maybe he gives up two goals in a 2-1 loss when he's faced 40 shots. I mean, it's happened this year. But even back then it had happened a couple of times. This was the opposite of that. He wasn't overly taxed throughout the game, until the third period.

"They get those opportunities and he was there for that. And in some ways that's even harder, because you're not as engaged in the game if you're stopping 14 shots as opposed to if you're stopping 38. So the fact he was there, locked in and ready for that moment (miraculous save on Thomas Vanek) in the third period, it wasn't surprising to me.

"Now I'll take you down to the final two minutes, because from like two minutes to around 1:30 they were peppering Hank. Montreal had it in the zone and the Rangers were unable to clear. They had their net empty from about 1:30 to go. Then, starting with like 45 seconds remaining there was a lot of neutral zone action. So it wasn't that nervous. Montreal couldn't get set-up after about the 1:30 mark.

"They didn't really get the chance to set-up in the zone and have a consistent attack on the Rangers. So that eased it up a little bit and it was just giddiness in the arena. The puck would cross the blue line and fans would get nervous, but the Rangers would clear it right away. And then the fans were back to being giddy. And the last minute largely played out that way. There wasn't this intense feeling like there was against Vancouver in 1994. After about the minute-and-a-half mark, the puck didn't spend a ton of time in front of Lundqvist's net. So that led to more giddiness then nervousness as the final seconds ticked off the clock.

"Then the final horn went off and that's the happiest I've ever seen Lundqvist. Here's a guy who's given Rangers fans so many great memories and made them happy on so many occasions. And just seeing the weight lifted off of his shoulders, like, he knew he was going to the Stanley Cup Final. He knew it was largely because of him. He was just so happy to finally have the chance to get to that level, because he had spent the first eight years of his career hearing, 'yeah, you put up great numbers, but you're not Marty Brodeur, you don't have the rings.' Well this was finally his chance to break through that and just the elation and the relief he showed is what I remember from that."

COMMENTARY FROM OTHERS AT THE GAME

DAN ROSEN: "There was a buzz. I mean it was a pretty distinct buzz, one that you hadn't seen around here for hockey in a while. I guess the buzz existed in 2012 when they played the Devils in that series. But I don't know, I got a feeling after they beat Pittsburgh; you just got that feeling like they were at least getting to The Cup Final.

"What I specifically remember was there was a lot of talk about Marty St. Louis, because the emotions and everything he went through. Just the fact he was going to play in Montreal, where he was going to be burying his mother. The whole team was going to be going to that funeral. If they had been playing somewhere else, what would have happened? And there was a lot of talk about Henrik (Lundqvist) because this was his moment. This was the time, finally. Again, they had that series in 2012, but the disappointment in 2012 I think might have fueled them in 2014 to fight, get over the hump and get to The Cup Final.

"I just remember it (Game 6) being tight and there wasn't a ton of opportunities. It was the type of Game 6 that kind of played like a Game 7, where neither team wanted to make the first mistake. That's kind of how I remember it. And I think it was the second period when the puck was bouncing all around in the neutral zone, Montreal came away with it and Thomas Vanek ends up with just an unbelievable 'Grade A' chance on his backhand. I believe the score was still 0-0. And Lundqvist just made that acrobatic, 'How In The World Did He Do That,' blocker save.

"He whipped his arm up, I think it hit off his pad or off his arm or shoulder and the puck popped up in the air. He whipped his arm up and bats it out of the air with his blocker. It was incredible. And then I remember going back, watching it and hearing Doc Emrick call it; which was really impressive to hear him call it. I think they went right to a commercial after that, but they showed the highlight.

"In the building it happened so fast. And then it went to commercial so you're not getting a great replay of it either. It was just a tremendous save. And then Dominic Moore scored, I believe it was late in the second period and Lundqvist didn't have to do a ton. I think he made 18 saves, but he made that huge save on Vanek and he shut the door.

"And then just the confetti falling (after the game was over) was just one of those magical Garden moments that that team in particular deserved. I think they earned it. I mean they had a lot of big moments and that was the biggest."

MOST UNFORGETTABLE RANGERS MOMENT

PAT O'KEEFE: "My most special moment covering the Rangers was on Vic Hadfield night at Madison Square Garden. I got to do a one-on-one interview during the second intermission with the man who's number had just been raised to the rafters. And that was incredible to me.

"The best anecdote he told me during the interview was the story about the day that he scored his 49th and 50th goals. He had torn ligaments in his thumb, to the point where he picked up a coffee cup in the coffee shop in the hotel and his thumb basically went down in the wrong direction. He was two goals away from becoming the first Ranger to ever score 50 in a season. They taped it up and he went out and played. He scored the goals and got the milestone.

"It was just the way he told the story to the media in the press room before the game. It was such a unbelievable illustration of how tough hockey players are that I felt the people listening on the radio should be able hear him tell it again, because just the way he told it was so matter of factly.

"It was like, 'Oh yeah, my thumb was hanging down so they taped it up. We had a game to play. It was no big deal. Yeah, it hurt. But I went out and I scored two goals anyway.' I mean that, to me, is just amazing.

It's just such an illustration of what these guys go through to play this sport."

11 HOWIE ROSE (WFAN)
GAME 7: 1994 EASTERN CONFERENCE FINAL (@MSG)
MAY 27, 1994
NYR 2, NJD 1

BACKGROUND

"Matteau behind the net ... Swings it in front ... He scores! Matteau, Matteau, Matteau! Stephane Matteau ... And the Rangers have one more hill to climb, baby, but it's Mount Vancouver! The Rangers are headed to The Finals!"

Every self-respecting Rangers fan knows where he or she was when that jubilant call came over the airwaves. And if you aren't old enough to have witnessed the now iconic call first hand, you have probably heard the story so many times that it feels like you were there. For Blueshirts fans, it is a moment that is forever ingrained in their memory banks.

And, for one Howie Rose, it was -- and still is to this day -- a chance to be forever linked to his boyhood team.

Howie Rose was born in Brooklyn, NY, and from an early age, he knew he wanted to be a sports broadcaster.

"I'd probably known from a very early age that I wanted to get into broadcasting on some level," said Rose. "It always appealed to me. But in terms of hockey, the Rangers and broadcasting hockey for the Rangers, that was all because of Marv Albert. I fell in love with the Rangers and with the concept of broadcasting hockey all at the same time through Marv. It was 1966, when I was 12-years-old. The 1966-67 season was the first time the Rangers were in the playoffs after about a five-year absence."

"They didn't really generate a whole lot of attention in the newspapers back then," continued Rose. "But, around mid-November of that 1966-67 season, they started to play really well and they were generating more headlines and getting more attention. Then, one night, I happened to be stumbling around the radio dial and I came across WHN, 1050 AM New York, and Marv was doing a Rangers game. I stayed with it and was absolutely blown away. I was just completely enthralled by the excitement of it; by Marv, his pace, inflection, and obvious love for the Rangers. I was sucked in from that very moment."

So, at the tender age of 12, Howie Rose already knew what he wanted to do with his life; quite the amazing feat considering most take years to figure out their future endeavors.

Following the 1966-67 season, in late August of 1967, Rose came up with the idea to create the Marv Albert Fan Club. And when he mentioned it to his friends they quickly came on board. And that's really where the story of Howie Rose begins to gain traction.

"I said, 'well, I guess we should get Marv's permission somehow,'" Rose recalled. "I looked up the phone number for WHN and called. The switchboard operator answered the phone and in my rather high-pitched adolescent voice, I said, 'is there some way I could possibly speak to Marv Albert? Please.' And the next thing I know, bang, he's on the line and I was nervous as all hell."

"I asked him if we could have his permission to start a fan club," said Rose. "He was so gracious and so generous with his time and his resources. He told us that if we ever wanted to come up and see WHN we could and if there's anything we needed to help make the fan club a success, he'd do it."

Whether it was sending photos to the new fan club or providing tickets to Rangers, Mets, or Yankees games, Marv Albert stuck to his promise. And a few years later, he would prove to be instrumental in starting Howie Rose's career. As Rose matured, Albert would listen to and critique his tapes. And as Rose tells it, Albert wouldn't just say, "This is good." Rather, he'd give constructive criticism of Rose's work. And that benefitted Howie greatly.

But the teacher-student relationship didn't stop there. In 1975 Rose formally began his career by working for Sports Phone. And two years later, he landed his first radio job with WHN, which had -- in Rose's words -- "been sort of Marv Albert's alma mater." Eventually, Rose began to build a name for himself. And when Marv's schedule began to cause him to miss some games, he would recommend Rose as his fill-in.

According to Rose: "because I had no track record, no resume of doing major league level play-by-play, it took a while for people at The Garden to kind of take a leap of faith on me. But Marv finally convinced them to do that."

Then, on January 24, 1985, Rose finally got to the chance to call his first Rangers game, a contest that they won 3-1 against the Detroit Red Wings. Ever since that night, Rose has been a fixture in broadcast booths across the New York sports scene. And along the way he became friends with many media members, including Sam Rosen, who Rose says was always glad to provide assistance early in his career.

So, it's only fitting that two of the most recognizable broadcasters in New York sports were both on the call for what many believe is the greatest playoff hockey game ever contested; Game 7 of the 1994 Eastern Conference Final between the New York Rangers and the New Jersey Devils.

While Rosen held down the television duties for MSG Networks, Rose was tasked with calling the game on radio for WFAN. And, it's important to remember that back then, during the 1993-94 season, the television and radio booths were on opposite sides of Madison Square Garden; a factor that would become extremely relevant later in the game.

MOST UNFORGETTABLE RANGERS GAME

From the very start of the 1993-94 NHL season, the New York Rangers and the New Jersey Devils battled it out for the right to be called "The Best Team In The NHL." And after a grueling 82-game regular season, the Blueshirts prevailed, edging out the Devils not only for the Atlantic Division crown, but also for the President's Trophy. However, the margin of victory wasn't all that big, a mere six points separated the two juggernauts.

And with both teams finishing the season in excess of 100 points, it was clear they were on a collision course. The only question was who would come out on top?

The Rangers did their part to secure an appearance in the Eastern Conference Final, disposing of the Islanders and Capitals in a handy nine games. Meanwhile, across the river, the Devils needed 13 combined games to finish off the Sabres and Bruins and punch their ticket to the Eastern Conference Final.

The stage was set for a classic confrontation. Both teams were in the same boat, four wins away from earning a trip to the Stanley Cup Final or four losses away from having to adopt the old Brooklyn Dodgers saying, "Wait 'Till Next Year."

As is the case in war, there are many battles and a singular victory does not determine the overall winner. So, when the Devils -- more specifically, Stephane Richer -- defeated the Rangers in double overtime to take Game 1, all was not lost for the Blueshirts. And they proved it by coming back to beat New Jersey 4-0 in Game 2; evening the series at a game apiece.

Game 3 is always the classic, "Swing Game," and another double overtime matchup ensued. Unlike in Game 1, the Rangers came out on top, courtesy of trade-deadline acquisition, Stephane Matteau. (Remember that name).

With a 2-1 lead in the series, New York saw Game 4 as an opportunity to put the Devils' Stanley Cup dreams on life support. But New Jersey wasn't ready to kick the bucket; winning the game by a score of 3-1. And two nights later, the Garden Staters gave their Big City counterparts a heart attack; winning Game 5 by a score of 4-1. And most importantly it gave the Devils a commanding 3-2 series lead.

With New York's dream of finally winning the Stanley Cup slowly fading away, captain Mark Messier saw fit to inject his team, and by extension the city of New York, with some much needed confidence. Messier boldly declared the Rangers would win the game. And that declaration spawned the now famous headline, "WE WILL WIN GAME 6!"

But the Devils weren't so eager to let Messier get away with his bold act, taking a commanding 2-0 lead into the middle of the second period of Game 6. A late period assist from Messier on an Alex Kovalev goal brought the Blueshirts within 2-1 heading to the third period. What happened next is something only a Hollywood movie producer could come up with as Messier delivered on his "guarantee" and recorded a natural hat-trick to send the series to a decisive seventh game at Madison Square Garden.

For Rangers fans, this was what Messier was brought to New York to do; lead the team to victory and end the 54-year Stanley Cup curse.

Would The Captain be able to author another glorious tale? Or would it take another individual to finish off New Jersey?

Ladies and Gentlemen, I give you, Howie Rose.

HOWIE ROSE: "It was a magical time that spring of 1994 in New York. You had the Knicks and Rangers going on a great run and there was a big game at The Garden seemingly every night and they were all aired on WFAN; I was so proud to be a part of it.

"You have to understand, part of my background was so deeply established as a Rangers fan that even though I go on the air and broadcast the games, hopefully with a very professional approach, in my heart I so terribly wanted the Rangers to win. It was quite a challenge to sort of subjugate my emotions as a fan and be the consummate professional one has to be in those circumstances. So, the day before or the morning of Game 7, I was hyper as can be; I couldn't sleep. I would walk around nervously, with all kinds of energy beyond anything that would have been considered the norm. I was just antsy as can possibly be.

"And what I always reflected on about the sort of preamble to that game was that the most painful loss I had ever endured as a Rangers fan was in 1971 when they lost the seventh game of the semifinals in Chicago to the Blackhawks. And I really thought, that was the first year I had season tickets; '70-'71. I really thought the Rangers were going to win The Cup that year, especially after the Bruins were knocked out by Montreal in the first round.

"So that seventh game in Chicago, to me, was for the Stanley Cup because the Rangers handled the Canadians well that season. Even though most of that came before Ken Dryden came up and changed everything for the Canadians. But I really thought that seventh game in Chicago was for The Cup. They end up losing it; it was a 4-2 final. It was really a 3-2 game with an empty net goal and I've just never gotten over it. They should've won that game. They never should have lost it. They never should have lost that series. That seventh game in Chicago in 1971 haunts me to this day.

"So, as I was getting ready to broadcast Game 7 against the Devils, it just kept coming back to me that this is that same game. This is Game 7 with a chance to go to The Final. This was just like that game in Chicago in '71 and very much the same to that seventh game in Philadelphia in '74, which they also lost by a goal. I said, 'man, those are two of the toughest losses I ever had to deal with as a Rangers fan and now I'm broadcasting a game that can kind of make good on all of it if the Rangers win.' So I was just so hyped up for the seventh game against the Devils.

"My broadcast partner was the Hockey Hall of Famer, Sal 'Red light' Messina, one of the all-time greats. I had probably done 55 or 60 games during the regular season out of the 84; I think they played that year. Marv had all those conflicts and even though I was technically his backup, I was the guy who did most of the games, so it was not unusual for me to be in that seat that night.

"So, there wasn't much to do in terms of preparation. After all, it was Game 7 and we had done six games before that. It was obviously a situation where the Rangers were given this gift of the win in Game 6, when Messier had the guaranteed hat-trick or made the guarantee that they'd win the game and he comes through with a hat-trick. I don't know that we felt like we were living on borrowed time with the Rangers, but we were on even terms with the Devils, which is the best they could have hoped for at that point.

"And so, my broadcast partner was Sal and we were jacked. I mean, it was one game to determine whether or not the Rangers were going to the Stanley Cup Final. You don't need to look to any external sources to get motivated to reach this sort of fever pitch that inevitably accompanies Game 7 because those two words, Game 7, are magical in it of themselves.

"It could have been Game 7 against anybody, but because it was the seventh game of the Conference Final with a chance to go to the Stanley Cup Final meant that the only challenge that I had, because I had to a call a game, was to keep my emotions in check. And that was the only thing that as a professional I felt that I needed to kind of check myself on from time to time during the game; don't get carried away. Don't sound like a fan and don't go over the top. Your professionalism hopefully takes over in a situation like that. And I hope mine did."

With Rose and Messina all revved up the Rangers managed to draw first blood, thanks to a highlight-reel goal by Brian Leetch in the second period.

HOWIE ROSE: "I remember the play. I think it was off a face-off when Leetch makes his move towards the net and then kind of spins around and puts a backhander by Brodeur. And I remember an absolutely fabulous heartfelt call by Sal Messina, somewhat incredulously, he said, 'that's a Bobby Orr play.' And it sure as heck was and I just was so blown away by the brilliance of the play. But it was 1-0. I don't remember exactly what time it was in the second period, but I know there was around half a game to go, so I wasn't counting any mileage to Vancouver yet. It was just nice that the Rangers took the lead.

"I could not allow myself to think 30, 40 minutes ahead. I just remember Sal nailing it, when he said, 'that's a Bobby Orr play,' and he couldn't have been any more on target with that."

Slowly but surely those 30 to 40 minutes were coming off the clock, and yet, the Rangers were still holding onto their 1-0 lead. But anybody who thought the game was going to end with that same score was sorely mistaken as the Devils' Valeri Zelepukin scored a dagger of a goal with 7.7 seconds remaining in the third period to tie the game at 1.

HOWIE ROSE: "First off, that's exactly what it felt like, a cruel and unusual form of punishment. It was a dagger to the heart when Zelepukin scored. What I remember thinking as we got inside the last couple of minutes was, 'if they hold onto this lead and win, then I just want to punctuate the game with something succinct and let the crowd carry it for a few seconds and then pick it up.'

"So in my mind, I thought, 'alright,' if you know, I don't remember when I started to think this, it wasn't very much before the last minute that I would say, 'and there's one more hill to climb' as the clock ran out and let the crowd take over and then rejoin. So you know, however things lead to Zelepukin scoring that goal, obviously when he scored the goal, there went the whole 'one more hill to climb' business.

"But what I remember most from Zelepukin's goal is that I always had a pen in my hand. Usually, I think it was in my left hand. I would hold onto it. It was sort of a nervous habit. I just kept that pen and didn't do anything in particular with it. It was just a little bit of a safety blanket, or I guess a security blanket the phrase is. But when Zelepukin scored, I mean you've got to realize that, they're inside the last 10 seconds on their way to the Stanley Cup Final and the Devils tie the game.

"Well, I took that pen and I just disgustedly flung it into the air and I figured, 'well it wasn't an expensive pen, just some little bit' and when I let go of the pen, I never imagined I'd ever see it again."

While Rose threw his pen, Mike Richter was down on the ice putting himself, and the Rangers, in a dangerous situation as he charged referee Bill McCreary in order to argue the play.

HOWIE ROSE: "I was so overwhelmed by rage, that the Devils had tied the game that I couldn't even recognize the precarious position that Mike put himself into there. I guess I saw it, but the devastation of having been scored on was so great that I couldn't even allow myself to think of ramifications of Ricky bumping into McCreary the way he did. That wasn't even on my radar and I know people made a fuss about it later on, but it wasn't even anything that I remotely considered in the moment, because we were all so consumed with the reality of Zelepukin having scored and the game having been tied.

"So they play the last 7.7 seconds, now we're going to overtime and I throw it to a break and I'm just despondent. I cannot believe this happened. I just thought, 'well, there's no way the Rangers are going to win this game. They never win games like this.' This is in perfect concert with the last 54-years and this is just the cruelest blow of them all and now they would probably lose. And, how can you ever believe ever, ever, ever that they're going to win?

"Well, I looked down at some point during that first intermission and I spent a lot of time looking down because my head was just bowed, but I saw the pen, I couldn't believe it. The pen landed. I mean I threw it straight up and I figured God knows where it was going to wind up. It landed right at my feet. I didn't know it until I looked down and there it was and I thought, 'maybe that's an omen,' and just sort of went on with my business."

Whether or not the pen returning was an omen is up for debate. But one thing that isn't debatable is how close the Devils came to winning the game when -- during the first overtime -- the puck went off Bernie Nicholls' skate and trickled past Mike Richter.

HOWIE ROSE: “I remember expecting that the Devils would somehow score because that fit the script that had been written over the last 54-years. I probably imagined every manner of ways that the Devils would score, however fluky they might've been and thankfully they didn't.

“The closest call I remember happened the second overtime. I remember Stephane Richer came in, had a great chance and Richter made a great save and the puck rebounded, seemingly right out towards the front of the net and stayed there for what seemed like forever, until, as I recall, Brian Noonan came away with it. That was as close a call as I remember.”

The Rangers were fortunate Noonan was in the right place at the right time. But he wasn’t the only Rangers player who was going to be able to claim that distinction.

When the Blueshirts took to the ice to warm up for the second overtime, they were missing a player; Stephane Matteau, who stayed back in the locker room in order to get his skate fixed. Once his skate was back to normal, Matteau headed out to the ice and on his way, he passed by the Prince of Wales Trophy.

NHL superstition dictates that nobody touches the trophy, even after they win it. And certainly not beforehand.

HOWIE ROSE: “Nobody wanted to go anywhere near the Prince of Wales Trophy. It’s a superstition that’s maybe been diluted over the years, but nobody wanted to go near that thing.”

But Matteau defied the superstition and touched the Trophy, perhaps hoping for some good fortune. And evidently it worked in his favor as Matteau scored what is now considered to be, one of the most iconic goals in Rangers history and possibly even NHL history. And along the way, Howie Rose was able to etch his name alongside Matteau’s, thus fulfilling his boyhood fantasy.

HOWIE ROSE: “We had the best vantage point in the building for that because our location on radio was right above the old tunnel that has been famously renamed The Willis Reed Tunnel, which is because of the story where Willis came out from the locker room before Game 7 of the 1970 NBA Finals.

“But because we were so far down, I could almost magnetically keep that puck attached to my eyes. So your powers of concentration are so sharp and so acute and so absolutely singular in situations like that that there was no separating my eyeballs from that puck. And so, as Matteau came around the net, all I saw was the puck in his stick blade. And interestingly after the goal was scored and after I finally started screaming, stop screaming, Sal is now talking over the replay and he's, for all of the fans, describing in detail what happened.

"Well, he saw Tikkanen crashed the net. And on the replay, Sal said on the air, 'you know, I don't know if that's not Tikkanen, I'm not so sure that's Matteau's goal. That might've been Tikkanen.' At that point my heart sunk and I'm thinking to myself, oh no, now I'm going to have to go into the studio and overdub, 'Tikkanen, Tikkanen, Tikkanen,'or something to that effect, thinking maybe Esa Tikkanen had scored the goal. But thankfully he didn't. That was Matteau's goal and I was vindicated because my eyes, all four of them were right on it.

"At that point it was sheer delirium and this image of Mount Vancouver jumped into my head and I don't know, to this day for certain, I think there is, if there really is a Mount Vancouver. It just popped into my head. As I say, the 'one more hill to climb' thing was something I had thought about. But once you go to overtime and you don't know who is going to score the goal and how it's going to be scored, you can't lean on anything you might've planned; you just go with the moment. And in the midst of my hysteria, the one more hill to climb thing jumped back into my head and then Mount Vancouver popped in there. I don't know how or why or from where or whom, but it did. And if that enriched the call, so be it. But it was absolute spur of the moment, maniacal, unabashed joy, no other way to put it.

"I'm really happy to be connected to Stephane because he's such a good guy. I mean, he's just a nice, nice man. And so I'm very proud to be associated with him as part of a moment that is so ingrained and important really to New York Rangers history. Apart from Stephane, I'm just incredibly, incredibly proud to have a tiny piece of the history of the New York Rangers connected to me personally because of how much I loved them growing up and having been a huge fan of theirs and later a season ticket holder and, of course, a broadcaster. Most guys in this business work their entire careers without having a moment like that at any time. And so the fact that I had one of those was improbable enough and is something in it of itself that makes me very happy.

"But, for me, if you look at my high school yearbook, you'd have thought that I played for the Rangers. People would say to me, 'Howie, good luck with the Rangers, the Rangers are going to win The Cup.' I cared so much about the Rangers and the Mets, that was my identity in high school. So, for me to be connected to such an integral part of their history and to be umbilically tied to a moment that is among the most memorable in the history of the franchise, it quite frankly just blows my mind."

COMMENTARY FROM OTHERS AT THE GAME

SAL MESSINA: "When you do a series like that, there's not a lot of preparation; maybe you talk to a player or two. It was kind of tense around the entire Garden and as far as preparing, it's just thinking back to the past games. It was, 'hey it's a chance to go to The Final.' Game 6 was a dramatic game as it was, with Messier calling, predicting they were going to win and coming through and getting that hat-trick. That line really meshed in the third period. There were two other overtimes in that series.

"It was a highly competitive series. I think Matteau scored an overtime goal in the series before that (in Game 3). And then the Devils also won a game in double-overtime (Game 1: Stephane Richer). Preparing for the game was really just, 'hey, it's a chance to go to The Final.' Don't forget, I was with the Rangers since 1963 in one capacity or another; all minor. And then I was a fan and had season tickets when I was 17-years old at The Old Garden. And that was probably what my concern was, 'hey we've got a chance to go to The Final.' As far as the preparation goes, it's just watching and talking about what's going on in the game. Both goalies were great. It was a goaltenders' game the way they played. I can't remember any distinct plays but I do remember thc competitiveness of the games.

"That's an overstatement really because how could they not be competitive games. There were ups and downs. In the third period the Rangers were holding onto a lead, but third period shockers by the Devils were just something you expected could happen. The game was just so competitive and it could have gone either way really. The goaltending for both teams was really good. I think both came up with great saves. It was a really tense, tense game. Our location was down low so you could really feel the emotion of the players.

"You're talking over 25-years ago now, and that series was just one thing happening right after the other. The place going silent (when Zelepukin scored with 7.7 seconds to go). There was a play before that which I remember being a little controversial as (Mike) Richter tried to clear the puck and the whistle was blown. Everybody was thinking the game was over at that point. Richter was clearing the puck, I believe, and the referee blew the whistle on the play and that set-up at that face-off. I remember saying to myself, 'Oh Wow!' And then the Devils scored.

"We were looking forward to The Final and then it was, 'here we go; another overtime.' The two of us (Howie Rose and I) looked at each other like, 'oh no, not again.' You're basically waiting for that overtime to start and then you have to do it again. I know I had a guest. What I used to do is I would prepare by asking a writer or somebody to be my guest for overtime. The play in the overtime, both goalies came up with some huge saves. I know Richter especially made some great saves. Both teams had some really good chances. But it was a goalies' series; both Richter and (Marty) Brodeur had been phenomenal.

"The rivalry and the emotions, every face-off, it was all 'oohs and ahhs.' Every save basically decided the series. Every shot that could have gone in, that was the series. That's how emotional it was and how exciting it was. Howie had to describe it and then I had to find some tidbit about it. We were really concentrating on that more than anything else. If you're just watching the game, you're watching the game. But I was concentrating on how to describe it.

"I think Matteau started along the far boards and just came around and I didn't expect it to go in. I believe it took a crazy hop over Brodeur's stick or something. Don't forget, we're down low and it looked like Brodeur made the save, but then it just trickled through. Howie made that terrific call and then I had to think of what to say after that. For Stephane Matteau, it was his second overtime goal of the series, which was incredible.

"The elation, I was the broadcaster for the Rangers, I had been with them my entire life, and we were going to The Final. Although, I did go to one other Final with the Rangers in 1979 against the Canadiens. You felt the Rangers had this chance to win The Cup. And Howie was just tremendous and an emotional guy and just a big, big Rangers fan. It's hard to believe he went to work for the Islanders afterwards, which I tease him about."

MOST UNFORGETTABLE RANGERS MOMENT

HOWIE ROSE: "I go back to my very first game on January 24, 1985, against the Detroit Red Wings. The Rangers score their first goal of the game and it was the first game I'd ever done. So, I thought it was an audition for any future games as a Rangers broadcaster and I sort of blew the call. What happened was, through a chain of circumstances that night, not only was I filling in as the play-by-play guy, but the 'Big Whistle' Bill Chadwick was filling in as well.

"He ended up in the booth working with me and he hadn't worked a game in some years, particularly on radio. And he was elaborating on something having to do with a referee making a call. So, Bill was telling me on the air that he was the referee who devised the hand signals that referees would use to indicate a penalty. And, because it was my first game, I wanted to be particularly respectful to Bill. So Bill made that comment about having devised the hand signal system for referees and I felt I needed to acknowledge that, even though he talked a little longer than he should have.

"When he was finishing his comment, they had already dropped the puck. So, because I was inexperienced and I was sort of being deferential towards Bill, I just threw a line out there. I think it was something to the effect of, 'well they say an artist's best work is never appreciated until he's gone,' or something like that. But in the five seconds or whatever it was that I wasted filling in that comment when it really didn't need it to be delivered, what do you know, they score. It was right off the face-off, Peter Sundstrom scores for the Rangers and you could hear the crowd react in the background before I say, 'Sundstrom scores.'

"I thought I was done. I said, 'oh my God, I just talked over a goal. It's the cardinal sin for a broadcaster, I'll never be invited back.' You might think it's a low point, but what made it memorable for me was that I had the wherewithal to forget about it and not dwell on it and then go back to calling the game. And I knew I called a good game. I really kind of felt afterwards that I nailed the game, but I knew I screwed that up and I was very afraid that would be a mistake that would cost me another opportunity to ever do a Rangers game.

"Luckily, the executive producer at the time, a very nice man by the name of Phil Harmon, at Madison Square Garden Network said, 'look, you know, Bill hasn't done this in awhile. He was really rusty and you know, he talked longer than he should have and I understand why you felt you had to say something. Don't worry about it. The rest of the game was great, we really were happy with it.' For what that meant to me, to be able to overcome that mistake and go on to do many, many hockey games after that is something I'm very proud of. It's like hitting a crummy shot on a golf course and being able to forget about it and go make the next shot a good one."

12 SAM ROSEN (MSG NETWORKS TV)
GAME 7: 1994 EASTERN CONFERENCE FINAL (@MSG)
MAY 27, 1994
NYR 2, NJD 1

BACKGROUND

The man known as, "The Voice of The NY Rangers," Sam Rosen has spent the better part of the last four-plus decades providing an unmatched level of professionalism, excitement and overall quality to Rangers broadcasts -- both television and radio.

The 2016 Foster Hewitt Award recipient and NHL Hockey Hall of Famer, Rosen has been a regular presence in the Rangers television booth since the 1984-85 season and he's still going strong today.

As a True Blue Rangers fan growing up in New York City, Rosen had ample opportunities to acclimate himself with Madison Square Garden; both old and new. And in 1970, that familiarity worked to his advantage, as he became the statistician for the NY Knicks Radio Network.

Then, in 1973, he joined UPI Radio Network, covering the Knicks and, of course, the Rangers.

"I would come to The Garden to cover Rangers games," said Rosen. "And a lot of it was doing post-game interviews, which we would use for the UPI audio feeds. But, during the course of covering those games, I would take out a period of time, usually the second period, or even part of the third period, and go off to a corner of the press box and record play-by-play on my tape recorder. And, basically, I used that as an audition file. Whenever I was in need of a play-by-play tape, I would use those recordings as part of my resume while looking for a job."

Sam stayed at UPI until 1980, but it was his time at WINS that put him on the path to becoming the broadcaster he is today. And that's where he met Jim Gordon.

"I was in college and also working for the New York Knicks Radio Network where he (Jim Gordon) was doing play-by-play," said Rosen. "And I got to know him very well. He was my mentor and he was the guy who listened to my tapes and critiqued my work."

"Then, in February of 1977, the Knicks were playing the Nets and Jim was supposed to fill-in for Marv Albert on Knicks radio," recalled Rosen. "But Jim got sick and couldn't do the game, so they asked Jim to recommend someone and he recommended me to do the game and I did; and I've been here ever since.

"And then, the following season, the question came from the people at MSG, 'could I do hockey?'" said Rosen. "So I took my tapes and handed them to them and said, 'yes, I can do hockey.' At that point, I became the radio backup to Marv Albert. Then, I believe it was the 1978-79 season, Jim was hospitalized with a back issue and was out of commission for a month, so I filled in on T.V. for him doing Rangers hockey. And then, in 1982 I signed my first full-time contract with MSG. I hosted Knicks' basketball, Rangers' hockey and was the fill-in on Rangers radio whenever Marv couldn't make a game.

"Finally, in 1984, MSG decided to make a change on the T.V. side and offered me the Rangers' job. The '84-'85 season was my first full season doing Rangers hockey on T.V."

Since that season, Rosen has witnessed an innumerable amount of iconic Rangers games and moments. Therefore, it's no surprise that the game which stands out most to him, is one that still sends shivers down the spines of New Yorkers everywhere: Game 7 of the 1994 Eastern Conference Final against the New Jersey Devils.

MOST UNFORGETTABLE RANGERS GAME

Few games in Rangers' history have been as hotly hyped and tightly contested as Game 7 of the 1994 Eastern Conference Final against the Devils.

When the Devils moved to New Jersey from Colorado prior to the start of the 1982-83 season, the franchise wasn't viewed as much of a threat to the Rangers. Infamously, they were called a "Mickey Mouse organization," by then Oilers' star, Wayne Gretzky.

But, by the early 1990's they had been built into a team that was to be reckoned with. And at the start of the 1993-94 season, they were ready to take the league by storm. However, the Rangers weren't quite ready -- or willing -- to step aside. Therefore, it was appropriate both teams spent the season trying to outdo the other in a fierce race to make the playoffs.

When the regular season came to an end -- and the dust from their battles had settled -- the standings read:

New York Rangers: 112 points

New Jersey Devils: 106 points

The six point margin of victory not only allowed the Rangers to win the Atlantic Division crown, but also the President's Trophy as the best team in the league. And just like they did in the division race, New Jersey finished with the second-highest points total in the entire NHL.

So, it was only fitting that the two best teams in the league met in the Eastern Conference Final; four wins away from going to the Stanley Cup Final, or four losses away from a devastating defeat.

When New Jersey jumped out to a 1-0 series lead at Madison Square Garden, courtesy of a double-overtime goal by Stephane Richer, the Devils looked poised to upend the favored Blueshirts and prolong New York's 54-year Stanley Cup drought.

But the Rangers weren't deterred; winning Game 2 at home by the score of 4-0.

From there, the New York squad took a 2-1 series lead in Game 3, thanks in part to a harbinger of things to come. Mid-season acquisition, Stephane Matteau scored a dramatic double-overtime goal against Devils' rookie netminder, Martin Brodeur to put the Rangers in the driver's seat.

However, New Jersey had no desire to lay down and roll over. The Devils recovered from the heartbreaking Game 3 loss to capture both Games 4 and 5 to put the Blueshirts on the brink of a way-to-soon elimination.

With the Blueshirts staring at a 3-2 series deficit entering Game 6, captain Mark Messier decided to give his team a confidence boost when he emphatically told the media, "We Will Win Game 6!"

But the Devils weren't impressed with Messier's bravado and carried a 2-0 lead into the midway point of the second period.

What happened next is the stuff of legend as a Messier assist brought the Rangers within 2-1 heading into the third period. And then, it happened! Messier recorded a third period natural hat-trick to stave off elimination, force Game 7 and deliver on his promise in the same way Joe Namath once guaranteed the Jets would win Super Bowl III and then delivered on his promise.

With the daunting pressure of Game 6 behind them, the Blueshirts turned their collective attention to Game 7.

"We felt okay," said Rosen. "A lot of the pressure had been relieved with the Game 6 win, because, you want Game 7 to be on home ice. Having won Game 6, and the way they won, it really invigorated the team. It was a great series that went back and forth and the Rangers knew the Devils were a team on the rise. They (the Devils) were a team that was probably right there; the Rangers' equal. I mean that series was as good as it gets. The games were close; having gone to double overtime in

Games 1 and 3. And, having won Game 6, the belief now was that it was ours for the taking."

How fitting? The two best teams in the NHL, playing a do-or-die Game 7 at The World's Most Famous Arena; 60 minutes -- or more -- away from a trip to the Stanley Cup Final.

Take it away Sam.

SAM ROSEN: "It was a Friday night at Madison Square Garden. And it was as tense and as nerve wracking an experience I've ever had. Of course, the series had gone back and forth. The Devils' won Game 1, and the Rangers won the next two before the Devils won, the following two. There was a tremendous, tremendous controversy in the Rangers' room with Brian Leetch being benched in Game 5, at New Jersey. Then Game 6 was the famous Mark Messier, 'We Will Win' game when he scored the hat-trick.

"We didn't do that game on MSG Network because we didn't do games in New Jersey and the Devils' could not have their broadcast done at The Garden. So, Game 7 is at The Garden, and it starts off with the Rangers and the Devils playing this tight, tight game. But the Rangers managed to score a goal in the second period (Brian Leetch at 9:31) to take the lead and they were trying to maintain the lead.

"Playoffs at The Garden were always so special. The crowd is just so intense and the building is just electric. In fact, the building even felt like it was vibrating and the crowd was on its' feet throughout the game. So, when Leetch scored, it just took things to a whole other level.

"Then you had Mike Richter, who was playing out of his mind; both goaltenders were great. But Richter was just fabulous. And in that game, the tension continued to build with the Rangers maintaining a 1-0 lead. It was getting closer and closer and closer to that moment. There were great chances throughout the game by both teams. And the Devils really had some great chances on Richter. But Mike made some fantastic saves to keep it 1-0.

"Then they were counting off the seconds. The Devils had pulled Brodeur and with 7.7 seconds remaining, Valeri Zelepukin scored and it was just crushing. I remember Richter came charging out of the crease at Bill McCreary and bumping him a little bit. But Billy being the great referee he was and understanding the situation, didn't give Mike a penalty. And you know, Mike was just beside himself, feeling he had been interfered with and there was no call on the play. But the Devils were all over the crease and Zelepukin put the puck in the net and we were headed for overtime.

"As the game unfolded, you saw it was going to be one play here or one play there that would determine if they were going to win 1-0. But with the seconds ticking off, the Devils found a way to tie the game. And from that point, it was basically one play to decide who was going to win the right to go to the Stanley Cup Final. And that play didn't come until the second overtime.

"So, we finished up the (third) period and threw it back down to Al Trautwig between the benches. And between the periods, before we went to overtime, I got out of my chair and sat down on the wooden platform in our broadcast booth, which held our game camera, and I just sat there shaking my head. John Davidson was walking, kind of pacing, back and forth. But then he looked at me and said, 'what's the matter?' And I said, 'what else can happen to this team?'

"I remember it being so quiet after Zelepukin scored and I definitely felt a sense of nervousness from the fans at the start of overtime. There was a nervous excitement because the crowd knew it could end any minute now; any second.

"It was just as if that moment was stolen from us. And sure enough, the naysayers and the people who believed in curses would somehow be right. Somehow, the moment the Rangers were going to reach The Final was going to be denied. Then the first overtime came and both teams had chances, but the goalies were brilliant. And I believe it was in that first overtime, there was a shot where the puck got knocked down and there were several bodies around the crease and I couldn't, see the puck so, I just blurted out 'where's the puck?'

"Finally, it was played into the corner and out of trouble. And then came the second overtime and of course, that magical moment. From our vantage point, there was Matteau with the puck coming in around the net and Esa Tikkanen going to the top of the crease with his stick down in the blue paint. Matteau wrapped the puck around and Brodeur was at the post trying to stop it with his stick down.

"And from our vantage point, it was hard to tell who got the goal, but it was just, 'the Rangers score!' and that unbelievable moment that they had made it to the Stanley Cup Final. It was just an incredible moment in time, where they had somehow come back and found a way to win Game 6 and overcome the tension, the pressure and the nervousness in Game 7. It was one of the greatest games ever played at The Garden and it put them in the Stanley Cup Final."

"To me, it was just one of those moments in sports that highlights a moment that will live forever. Stephane Matteau was one of the lead acquisitions during the season that Mike Keenan really wanted. He wanted that combination of Matteau and (Brian) Noonan; hard working players. Matteau had good size, and Noonan had the skills. Those were the type of gritty players Keenan wanted. And Matteau turned out to be this huge hero. He hadn't distinguished himself as a star player, although he was certainly a good player. But what he did in that series against the Devils; it was incredible.

"He had great moments in that series; like the double overtime goal in Game 3 and, of course, the double overtime winner in Game 7 to put the Rangers in The Final. Those are moments you can't script and for him, they secured his place in Rangers history. He'll always be remembered for putting the Rangers in the Stanley Cup Final with that goal.

"And I remember, the next day, being in the trainer's room at the practice facility and everybody just sitting around trying to collect themselves."

With their defeat of the Devils complete, the Blueshirts needed all the rest they could get, because their date with destiny -- not to mention the Canucks -- was rapidly approaching.

COMMENTARY FROM OTHERS AT THE GAME

JEFF BEUKEBOOM: "Well, obviously the tying goal, I was on the ice for that. I tried to clear it and didn't get it out and they scored with 7.7 seconds left on a goal by Zelepukin. So, that was a little deflating. But we regrouped, and tried not to let it phase us. Then obviously with Matteau, I was on the ice for that also. I remember getting the puck in, it might have been just before he scored and then they turned it over and Steph jumped on the rebound and then obviously we know how the goal went in. I remember being on the ice for that."

MIKE RICHTER: "We had had enough close games in that series. We had another double overtime in that series which we won in Jersey. That was Matteau as well (Game 3) which people forget. And during these games, there's an ebb and flow of whose got momentum. You get a read for how the refs are going to be. When Leetch scored in the second period, as a team you know you just can't hang on. You can't just hang your hat on one goal because anything can happen; a bad bounce and all of a sudden it's tied. So you still have to play the game and still try to score. And New Jersey was a good team at shutting you down.

"We also knew we probably weren't going to get a lot of goals, Brodeur's a fantastic goalie. The good news was, they had to play from behind the rest of the game and that's not their forte. They like to get a lead so they can shut you down from that point. So, they had to take some chances. You knew they were going to. They weren't going to go away quietly, so you still have to play a real structured game. The tendency is to hope time runs out quickly and just, you can't force that.

You have to play. You still have to go out there and play the rest of that shift, and pray you don't get scored on.

"The rest of that period we had to regroup and just wait for the kitchen sink to be thrown at us. If you sit back and are passive you will be playing catch up the whole time. It'll be trouble. If you get too aggressive, you open yourself up for problems. So, you really have to be a disciplined team and we're talking about that in the locker room and went out and played a good third period.

"By then, both teams are tired. You've had a long season; you've had long playoffs. It's been 10 days of playoffs with this team and you're into end of May now; guys are tired. So, the onus is on them to come back. The flip side, is they're in the away building; if they don't push back, their season's over there. They're going to have to take chances and they will and they've got great players on their team. They're going to be released a little bit from everything defensively and they're going to have to get guys like Zelepukin a chance to score. What does it mean? It means it's coming to the net. They're going to try to whack a puck in one-way or another.

"I thought we did a really good job of controlling as much as we possibly could. They had some very physically strong forwards who worked well down low and their defensive groupings were great about getting the puck to the net. You've got Niedermayer, who's so good at slipping in, like Leetch and just somehow becomes invisible.

"So at the end of that game, you know, as time is coming down, you're trying to keep that discipline. I made a save and there's a hesitation because there wasn't a Devil too close to me and you want time to move on. So I went to play the puck and I thought there was a very fast whistle. But, you know, if that's the way we're playing it. That set up another few face-offs in our zone. On the Zelepukin play when it went back you knew he was coming to the front of the net; I felt him there. But you have to take your eyes off him for a moment because the puck is in the corner and you need to watch it. When it came out in front, I read the play and made a save and he got one whack at it, two whacks and the third one, as I recall, went in.

"I felt like the puck was underneath me and had the whistle been as fast as it was the previous time the play would have been over. New Jersey wouldn't have liked that at all and I understand that. I just quickly popped up because the play prior to that they blew the whistle immediately, so why the long hesitation this time?

"I was just losing my marbles because we had lost our lead at the end of the game. My argument was, just consistency in terms of when you blow the whistle. Billy McCreary is a great guy and a great ref, and whether he lost sight of it and didn't know whether it was full or not, whether he saw him whacking it and thought that it was free, you know, he's a professional. He gets to make his judgment. But I was heated and I came over and I just told him, 'I had it under me, you can't leave him whacking it away like that.'

"And I was in a position where I had no leverage to get my upper body over and cover it, but I had it under my leg, I thought. Anyway, he clearly didn't see it that way, but I think, to his credit and my good fortune, he just got out of there. Later I came out for that overtime period and of course we were all upset and devastated. But he said, 'Mike, I understand you got a little heated there and emotions are a little raw right now with both teams. So I just decided to get out of there.' And I was happy he did because he could have thrown the book at me and he didn't. So that means the veteran referee understands the situation and he made a call that, I don't think it was a bad call, I was just upset with it at the time. He was good enough to not rub it in my face and give me a penalty at that moment; because I clearly came out of my crease to give him my two cents.

"You definitely go into those things (overtime periods) knowing that a lot of times it isn't a Brian Leetch going from end to end and shooting it under the crossbar. A lot of times, someone does a turnaround shot and chucks it to the front of the net and it hits your own guy or something and bounces off the goalie, whatever it is. They can be pretty ugly.

"I mean, you guard against good plays; clearly you have to. These guys are capable of making great plays, but when you get to a seventh game, double overtime, any little battles can end your season. And it seems a shame to have it that way, but our two teams were so tight that anything can happen and that's why you get pucks to the net. You have more of a chance of it dinging off of somebody, or the goalie just missing it or never seeing it.

"For years people would say, 'overtimes are won in the first few minutes.' Well, this one didn't happen that way, right? I mean it went into the second overtime. So you had this rhythm of the game where obviously you're dialed into focusing on who's on the ice, who's coming out and what the situation is. But as part of the position you do a little bit of, I don't want to say spectating.

"When it's 200 feet down there, and you're watching Marty do his thing and we're trying to score, you try not as a goaltender to say, 'I hope we score,' because we may not. We may not even get a shot off. Or we might have 10 great shots and Marty makes 10 great saves. You just have to worry about when they're shooting.

"But when (Matteau) went behind the net, just the way it occurred; it was so intense with everybody watching it. The focus was so great in the arena; you get this tension in the air and every shift matters. It could be the end of the season right there. You've come so far and you have so much promise and you think you're going to do it, but nobody knows. That's why you play sports. That's why it's compelling. And it's so awesome to be part of that. I mean, you just dialed in like as much as you possibly can be. Everybody on the bench, the trainers, they're all on their toes.

"And, you know this game will end, you just don't know when. It goes that first five minutes in the first overtime and then you're halfway through and you're in a rhythm. Then it's the last little bit and everybody makes their press. And then before you know it, you're going to the second overtime.

"It looked like the puck could have come out once or twice there and somebody shot it back in. Then Stephane does what Stephane does. He's great in the corner, he's strong, he's smart, he knows where to go and it's overtime; it's the seventh game. You get it in front of the net, you have teammates there. That's the whole idea. If you see Tikkanen standing there, and when he went around the net, Marty went down and Fetisov slid over, but from my angle of it, there was this hesitation when Marty was kind of reaching with his left leg extended. Then there was just a pause and it seemed to me a moment where everything just stood quiet and still. And I was like, 'I think that went in.' But I didn't hear a roar.

"I was expecting to be told there was a goal by the crowd more than see it go in and I had enough time to think that it looked like it went in, but I wouldn't even let myself go there because that means you let your guard down; the game's over, you've won, you're going to The Finals, all the things we want to do.

"And it was quite. Even Stephane had to almost recognize it was in and Marty had to find out it was in and you can see that in the body language. And then, just the place, it was like an explosion and all of a sudden you're back to real time. But back to that moment, I literally had a moment in my head and I think the puck went in, but I heard no noise. So you almost reacted to the, to the lack of reaction from the fans saying, 'oh, it must not have been.'

"And BOOM, the place just exploded. You almost don't let yourself go there. And then Marty slumped down and Fetisov slumped down. Stephane is doing is war dance there and Tikkanen and it just was absolute pandemonium and it's, all that pent up focus and energy and effort gets released at that moment and it was just awesome. Just so much fun to be a part of."

MOST UNFORGETTABLE RANGERS MOMENT

SAM ROSEN: "It's hard to pick just one (moment). But when you win a championship, in any sport, and you're a part of it and close to the people who are involved in winning it, namely the players, that has to be the ultimate moment. That's what every athlete strives for no matter what level. I remember doing it as a kid; playing in school or in tournaments. You just wanted so badly to win. Being around professional athletes, who make a lot of money, but they want to win so badly; that's what drives them.

"They really want to win. And when you see these athletes achieve that ultimate success, and as I mentioned before, being around it; that's the ultimate moment. And seeing the Rangers win the Stanley Cup for the first time in 54-years, at Madison Square Garden and being a part of that whole scene and the whole season leading up to it, that's my ultimate moment.

"There were tremendous, dramatic moments that happened during the course of the season. It started with a trip to London to play the Toronto Maple Leafs in the French's Mustard Cup in September of 1993. And then the team going on a 20 game unbeaten streak. Then there was the team coming together and the star players and the big trades at the deadline where some of those star players, I keep thinking about Mike Gartner being traded or Tony Amonte being traded.

"But then it all came together in that drive for the Stanley Cup. And how hard it was to win the series against the Devils. Then, being up 3-1 against Vancouver and then having to go to a seventh game to win the Stanley Cup. It's fantastic to be a part of it and to be around it and the memories last a lifetime. It's just unbelievable. That is the snapshot, winning the Stanley Cup and then seeing the celebration at The Garden and the celebration in the streets of New York and the celebration on that Friday, when the team was honored in the Canyon of Heroes. It doesn't get any better."

MESSAGE TO RANGERS FANS

KENNY ALBERT: "I want to compliment Rangers fans because they are the most passionate in all sports. When you talk about their knowledge of the game, their history, and knowing the history of the organization; I just think you won't find that type of passion in too many other places.

"So, my message would be to keep coming out to The Garden. These are great fans and it's now the next generation. Most of the people in this building today, probably weren't here in '94. But keep bringing the passion and rooting for the team on the ice and hopefully they can win another cup in the very near future."

JEFF BEUKEBOOM: "From my perspective, it would be the fact that we were able to deliver that victory that championship to the fans, who were so rightfully deserving. Until you've been around those fans, played for those fans and talked to many of them, you don't realize how passionate and how great they are. Some of them are lifelong and generational fans that just kept passing down through their families. To be able to deliver to them that opportunity, that championship, I'm speechless. I can't say words that mean enough to all of them."

LARRY BROOKS: "Just enjoy it when the team plays well because it doesn't last forever. I know when I was growing up and rooting for the team that never won; the Emile years. There was always disappointment at the end of the year. But it is always better to be good, come close and feel the pain of losing than it is to be an irrelevant team, when games in January, February, March and April mean nothing. Coming close and not winning is tough, but coming close and not winning, is a lot better than not coming close."

RICK CARPINIELLO: "Rangers fans have every right to be pessimists. They are a team that has been through hell and back. There are other teams in the city that have had miserable stretches, some of them haven't won anything in a long time, but the Rangers fans stick by their team more than the other fans. Now, when I say stick by, it doesn't mean they're not negative, because they are negative and they get apoplectic when they lose a period, never mind a game. They get crazy when they lose one in a row after winning nine.

"That's the nature of being a Rangers fan. But that's also what makes them so remarkable, is that they do stick by the team no matter what; no matter how bad it gets. And it gets bad sometimes. But then the other thing I know about them is they appreciated it when it happened in 1994; and I was in that parade. I was in a garbage truck. The Rangers put us writers in a sanitation truck ahead of the players so we could chronicle the parade.

"It was just remarkable seeing the Rangers fans and how they reacted. I saw a sign that said, 'my grandfather, thanks you. My father thanks you. And I thank you.' So, they'll still celebrate that day as long as they live; and some of them may not live for the next one. But they are the craziest, nuttiest, most loyal fans in New York. And I can't speak for other teams in other cities, but in New York, there's nobody else like them."

JOHN DAVIDSON: "Thank you for letting me a part of New York; I grew to love it. Thank you for, allowing me as a player to get to at least one Stanley Cup Final in '79 with a great group of players. Thank you for the support when I first moved to New York from smaller areas of the world. It's a very different world, but I grew to absolutely love it.

"When I look back at my life, I'm 65-years-old now, the greatest years of my life, by far in terms of being away from my family, was in New York. It was a very special time. They always say, 'if you can make it here, you can make it anywhere.' I don't know what I made, but I know one thing, I lived a very special life in New York City and I owe it to New York to say thank you."

JOHN DELLAPINA: "I guess my message is, and it's one my dad taught me growing up rooting for terrible Yankees and Giants teams, and myself cause I was a self made hockey fan; my dad really wasn't, watching the Rangers come close so many times. You have to go through the ride while it's happening, win or lose, because when it ultimately happens, it's so much better.

"If you haven't lived through the losses and you haven't watched them and you haven't gone to the games and you haven't stuck with your team through the bad seasons, you don't get to celebrate to the level that those people did that night at The Garden; and again two weeks later.
"I'll never forget two weeks later, when they finally won, and I'm

running down to do one of the five stories I had to do that night. And I had about 10 family members at the game that night who had tickets and they're crying. It took me back to being 12-years-old playing roller hockey in the cheese box in Astoria. That's what being a Rangers fan is."

STAN FISCHLER: "In my lifetime, I spent a lot of emotion rooting for the Rangers, starting with the Fan Club in 1950-51. We missed the playoffs in '51 after going to The Final in '50, a seventh game, double overtime. We missed it in '51-'52, '52-'53, '53-'54 and the year I worked for them in '54-'55. Then in '55-'56, they started to get things together. Particularly, when I was in the Fan Club, and I was sitting in the End Balcony, I was very, very emotional. And when I worked for the team I was very emotional.

"I remember coming home at midnight and my Mother saying to me, 'why are you throwing the newspaper against the couch?' I said, 'because we lost.' It was that way for a long time. I can relate to the most intense, craziest fans, because I did crazy things. I once threw not one, but two tangerines at referee Red Storey from the End Balcony. The first one missed, it was a tracer. I did it because he didn't call a penalty when Eddie Coleman of the Rangers had gotten slashed. I can relate to every fan's emotions because that's the way I was. To this day, none of that emotion has gone, except I'm not rooting for the Rangers like I used to.

"I rooted for the Rangers as long as I worked for MSG, because they're like sisters. But I can relate to all of this and my message to the fan is to relate to me the way you relate to the team now; and then you'll understand my feelings as I've described them. Hockey will always be the most emotional game. I played it a lot, very emotionally. And I write about it to this day emotionally. It doesn't go away. My message would be what Red Dutton's message was in his book, to 'Keep Punching.' And that's what I say to fans, 'enjoy the game and keep punching.' Just don't be as crazy as I was."

JOHN GIANNONE: "So, 1977 was the first time I ever walked into The Garden for a Rangers game and I was 14-years old. I had gotten a Christmas gift, two tickets to a Rangers-Sabres game, and it's a moment that still stays with me. My dad and I took the Long Island Railroad from Jamaica, Queens, we lived in Flushing, and we got upstairs and the first thing I marveled at was the ice was on the sixth floor or maybe the fifth floor.

"It didn't make any sense to me that a sheet of ice could be five floors above the street or what could be below it. I couldn't fathom any of that. I could never have thought that 30-years later, I'd be working in a studio that's right below the ice at Madison Square Garden. Or that I'd be standing between the benches at every single Rangers game at

Madison Square Garden, which makes it a lifelong dream job. That first game in 1977, just the sights and the sounds and even the smells. Just what The Garden meant and what the Rangers meant.

"I had just sort of transitioned my fandom from one team to another. A team that will remain nameless in these parts. But when I was a much younger kid, when I first got into hockey, I was a Flyers fan because I had gotten an AM Radio from my mom for Christmas when I was nine and I'd go to bed by trying to get radio stations from different cities. And one of them I got was Philadelphia. And I heard Gene Hart call a game and I immediately fell in love with his voice, with what he was saying, with how the game sounded and therefore the team he was calling.

"Therefore, I was a Flyers fan up until 1977 when they started trading away their two Stanley Cup champion players. And I switched my allegiance to the Rangers. Also because, at that point, I was pretty much going to high school and a lot of my friends were Rangers fans, so I shifted to becoming a Rangers fan. And once I came into this building for the first time, it stuck with me forever. What I know about Rangers fans is they are the most passionate, the most knowledgeable and the most loyal fans of any team I've ever been around or that I've ever covered. And that is the same to this day. Virtually all of the Rangers fans of this generation watched games with their dads growing up. And their dads watched games with their dads growing up.

"And that's what Rangers hockey here at The Garden represents. It's the level of passion the fans bring, not only to coming here for every game, but now in this 21st century generation of social media and social interaction, the level of passion they bring on Twitter, on Facebook, and on Instagram and in social media circles, so when I see that, it makes me realize just how important the Rangers are to the fabric of sports in this city. It's something where I think the message would be, 'thank you.' 'Thank you for bringing the level of passion you do to every game, because it certainly makes what I do, a labor of love."

ROD GILBERT: "Hi, this is Rod Gilbert, saluting all the Rangers fans and I want to acknowledge their passion and their support for the Rangers teams through the years. My goal is to meet all the Rangers fans, whether it's at The Garden or a charity event, or even on the street. Please say hello and introduce yourselves and let me thank you personally. Be blessed and have a great time and LET'S GO RANGERS!"

ADAM GRAVES: "For me it was just the privilege of wearing that jersey. Being on The Garden ice and playing in front of those who are Rangers fans. In one word it was a privilege. And that privilege extended into the community after games, in the off-season and during the season.

"It was a very special bond that I'll always, always, always hold close to my heart and I consider myself very fortunate and privileged to have had the opportunity to be a part of the bigger Rangers family. To the fans, to all my teammates, to the journey we took together through the '90s and still to this day. I just consider myself very, very fortunate."

ALLAN KREDA: "Rangers fans, they're famous and cerebral. They deserve credit for keeping the faith. That would be would the hash tag if there were a hash tag to apply. There are many, many fan bases who are similar and have similar mindsets in other sports. My sense is, we're not in Canada, so it's not as religious an experience as it is to be the fan of the Canadiens, the Leafs, Flames, Oilers or Canucks.

"The Rangers' thing is unique. They're an Original Six franchise with decades of frustration, near misses, not so near misses, bad teams and great teams who came close. It's a New Yorker meeting a dedicated fan, which is rare. The message is always the same; keeping the faith."

DON LA GRECA: "Just appreciate it. It's an amazing organization with a tremendous history. To walk into that building, which is now officially the oldest building in the National Hockey League, and to see the numbers in the rafters and see the connection the fans have with those players. I saw it from being a Devils fan growing up, to now working with the Rangers. I've seen it from both sides that it's not a fly by night kind of, 'oh we're hot, people love us. Or, oh we stink, nobody cares.' The building is always full. The fans are always passionate.

"They've always connected with the players; whether it's (Eddie) Giacomin to (Adam) Graves, to (Mark) Messier, to (Mike) Richter, to now, Henrik Lundqvist or Mats Zuccarello. They just appreciate that this is a family that's connected to its history; not just to their own history, but the history of the League and whether it's in a losing season or a winning season. It's a tradition that continues to march forward that really connects family and generations. And there are not a lot of organizations that can say that. And as much as you want to win, ultimately you know that when you're a fan of that team, you're part of a family and a tradition that's lasted for going on a hundred years.

"It's easy to follow a team that's going to win a championship every decade, or a couple. But it's one thing to say you can be that passionate about a team that's literally won one championship in 70-plus years. You're not going for the winning and you're not going because it's an easy team to root for. You're going because you appreciate the history and you appreciate the organization. Think about it, Kenny's (Albert) been doing games forever. Sam (Rosen) has been doing games forever. This is just a very comfortable organization to be around; at least for me anyway. They welcomed me with open arms and they treat me very well."

DAVE MALONEY: "Enjoy the competition and enjoy the experiences of being part of a clan or a tribe where you're going to have your ups and downs. There's no player who ever suits that goes out there not wanting to be the best they can be and despite how on some nights that best isn't quite as what it was maybe the night before. But being involved in the community and live and die with your team. That's part of what it's all about. I think those are the messages; enjoy the competition, root hard, take the losses hard, but as Freddy Shero used to say, 'it's only hockey.'"

SAL MESSINA: "Be as passionate as you've always been. Rangers' fans are always so passionate and great; just stay that way and things will change, they always do. It's tough to win a Stanley Cup. But stay as passionate and true as they always have been."

JOE MICHELETTI: "I've been fortunate enough to be in a lot of buildings and around a lot of different hockey fans. I have never been around a group of fans -- and I take the subway a lot, so I see a lot -- and they're good people. They're kind people and all they want to do is win. That's all they want to do. And I would say, 'don't ever lose that.' Don't ever lose that because that's what they know and that's the way I've always thought too; you win.

"We're trying to be try to be the best broadcast out there, we want to be better than anybody. And so, we hope that our fans think that. There's a connection there. And so, what's been established at Madison Square Garden Networks is a level that we hold ourselves accountable to. At times, we drift from there but then we catch ourselves. Right from the top on down they give us the most opportunity with the most cameras and the best people. And then they let us go work. I hope with our fans, that there's a connection there, between what they want and with what we want and that it works.

"There's going to be, and I hope I'm still here for it, a time when that Cup is carried around that ice again. I don't know when that's going to be, but I sure like what I see and what they're trying to do and build. So, stay passionate and our crew will stay passionate with what we do and that's a good combination."

PAT O'KEEFE: "I'll start off with a bit of a cliché, but I'm not going to finish with this. They say Rangers fans are more passionate than any other fan base in New York and I honestly believe that's true. There aren't as many of them, but those that are there are the most passionate fans in all of New York.

"I have this vision in my head of walking on the Chase Bridge to our booth with Dave Maloney, our color commentator, and he can't walk five-feet without middle-aged men coming up to him, just wanting to say hello and wanting to take their picture with him. It just amazes me to watch this every single time. Just showing how much he and this franchise, cause that's what he's representing, mean to this group of people of all ages. That's my takeaway of Rangers fans."

MIKE RICHTER: "I run into fans all the time now, I was just talking to a friend about this, and these people have supported the Rangers for damn near a century. For decades they've been in the same building. When you're drafted, playing and when your career is over, they're there. My message is absolutely simple. People say thank you to me, I want to say thank you to them. There's never a bad place to play this sport for a living.

"I would have been honored to play in the NHL in any city, but there's no better place than New York. And there's no better place to win in anything. I have to pinch myself sometimes. Just looking back, saying 'oh my God, I ended up in Manhattan playing for the Rangers, an Original Six team, winning the Stanley Cup with the greatest group of guys in the world in front of the greatest fans you could ask for.'

"We just came from Vic Hadfield with his night where his jersey went up to the rafters. And what's so compelling about that is the amount of gratitude he has. I've got to say the same thing. What makes an event like that special is the fans, the people who come to The Garden. It's a tightknit family every time you step out on the ice. The support they gave when we were winning The Cup and even when the team is rebuilding this year. They're unreal fans, they know the sport and they're great humans.

"People who come here from different places have one idea of New York and then they meet a Rangers fan and it's a very different thing. What makes it incredibly gratifying is the people you represent. I just want to say 'thank you' for all the support they've given us; it's been overwhelming. I think we all agree, it's such an honor to represent such a cool city and such good people."

HOWIE ROSE: "Well, what I would say to Rangers fans reflects on my formative years as a Rangers fan and probably fits the formative years any fan has with any team they adopt and carries on as a fan with for many, many years. The Rangers just retired Vic Hadfield's number and Vic's team, Emile Francis's team, were the team I fell in love with when I became a Rangers fan. The impact all of those guys had on me, whether it was the entire GAG Line, Eddie Giacomin, Brad Park or Walter Tkachuk, those were my guys.

"When the Rangers won The Cup in '94, even though it was Mark Messier and company who, won that Cup, it felt so good because of the memories that were made by the players who were there when I fell in love with the sport and particularly, the Rangers. It eats me up to this day, because I got to work with Emile Francis a little bit in that 1994 season. Again, string of circumstances, people were away for various reasons and I think I did two or three games with Emile. And what a thrill that was for me, because he was everything good about the New York Rangers, Emile Francis was.

"And my heart bleeds for him that he didn't win The Cup and that Rangers' team didn't win The Cup. But my love for the Rangers and for hockey was created by the success his teams had that year. I remember emceeing an event, I guess it was at the alumni golf outing the summer the Rangers won The Cup, so in probably September of 1994. There were a lot of Rangers alumni in the room that day or that night and many of them were the guys that I just spoke of. And I said, 'look, we're all thrilled that Mark Messier Brian Leetch, Mike Richter, Adam Graves and the rest of them got it done, but the reason that Cup means so much to us is because of so many of you among the alumni who were here tonight, like Rod (Gilbert), Jean (Ratelle), Vic, Brad, Walter, Eddie and all those guys.'

"I said, 'what you accomplished by drawing us in and by making us fall in love with the Rangers and hockey is why winning the Stanley Cup in '94 means so much to us now. You guys might not have been the ones to seal the deal, but the passion we have for the sport and for the Rangers directly is because of the success you guys had all of those years.'

"And that's really my message. Whatever generation you were a part of when you became a hockey fan, embrace that team and embrace those memories because that's what makes you love the sport and love your team the way you do today. So that's why whenever I see any of those players from that era and some of those I've gotten to know over the years, even to this day, all those years later and these guys are all in their 70s now and some are even approaching 80. They are still 10 feet tall to me and I'll be forever indebted to them for giving me the love of not only hockey but the New York Rangers."

DAN ROSEN: "Always appreciate Henrik Lundqvist for everything he's done for this franchise. His number 30 is going to go up in the rafters very much like Patrick Ewing. He may never win the Stanley Cup but he should not be defined by that. He should be defined by his consistent excellence almost every game. I say almost because goaltenders will have bad games every now and then. But almost every time he has gone in between the pipes at The Garden, or on the road, wearing a Rangers sweater, he has given his team a chance to win, if not he's been the best player in that game the reason his team won.

"He may never win the Stanley Cup but he's a Hall of Famer. He's one of the best of all-time. I think some people lose their appreciation of Lundqvist because he hasn't won The Cup, or they take for granted what he has done for this franchise. He's the best player in franchise history and he should be remembered as such; now, the day he retires, the day his jersey goes up to the rafters and 20 years from now, whether he's got a Cup or not."

SAM ROSEN: "My message would be to keep loving the team. I think the one thing that I had as a kid, and growing up as a fan, the one thing that I've tried to maintain, is my love for the team. And I think that's what fans have had. I think of all the years of going to the broadcast booth, before the building was redone, and talking to fans in the Blue Seats and how much they just wanted the reassurance that the team had a chance; that this team had a chance to advance and that this team somehow might find a way. I'm a positive guy and I always found the good things in every season and every year. But it's the love of the team and the love of the game and what the Rangers have meant to New York City through the years.

"They are part of the fabric of the city. And, yeah, there had been low moments when the team didn't make the playoffs for years. But there have also been great times when the team had strong runs and had a chance, like in 1994 when I said, 'And This One Will Last A Lifetime!' But the timeless message is to keep loving the team. It's a big part of sports in New York City and will always be that way. And there'll be good moments and there'll be tough moments; but just keep loving the team."

DEREK STEPAN: "Blueshirts fans are the most loyal, energetic group and they bring it every single night."

AL TRAUTWIG: "My message would be admiration for the passion they feel for the team. The number of faces I see on the loading ramp on 33rd street everyday, every game, all the time, every year, win or lose; waiting for Henrik to get in his car to drive home, waiting for everything Rangers. I'll just say, I admire their religion, because that's what it is to me.

"These people have the same dedication, love, admiration, adulation, commitment that they do on Sundays when they go to Church or when they go to Temple or whatever they do. And I just admire it. I just keep it in the back of my mind every single time I come on the air."

ACKNOWLEDGEMENTS

As famous Folk-Rock artist, Joan Baez wrote, "No man is an island, no man stands alone." And this book is no different. Therefore, I would like to acknowledge the following people for their roles in this project.

"The Hockey Maven," Stan Fischler, was a mentor of mine and helped me put this book together, not just through editing but by also allowing me to interview him for a chapter.

Sam Rosen, Joe Micheletti, John Giannone, Dave Maloney, Kenny Albert, Pat O'Keefe, Don La Greca, Allan Kreda, Rick Carpiniello, John Davidson and Howie Rose all took time out of their busy schedules to be interviewed for chapters in this book and told their stories with the same enthusiasm they share with the fans while doing their jobs.

Al Trautwig, Mike Richter, Adam Graves, Derek Stepan, Sal Messina, Rod Gilbert, Jeff Beukeboom, Dan Rosen, John Dellapina and Larry Brooks all provided their own color commentaries for the stories in this book.

Greg Dillard, Ryan Watson and Dan Schoenberg all helped provide access to the subjects of this book.

Mark Rosenman guided me through the process of self-publishing this book. And Elana Yavetz helped design the cover.

My parents -- Mandi and Seth -- sister -- Tara -- grandparents -- Morton, Stanley, Yvonne and Zella -- uncles -- Andrew, Lenny, Scott and Glenn -- and aunts -- Yvonne, Anita and Brooke -- all provided support throughout the book writing process.

My friends -- Arianna Rappy, Stef Hicks, Leanna Gryak, Maggie Wince, Brittany Ciraolo, Michele Rosati, Taylor Chiaia, Amanda Sorrentino, Jessica Sorrentino, Samantha Bruno, Maria Koutros, Walt Bonne, Daniel Greene, Jared Fertig, Brandon Dittmar, Landon Goldfarb, Joey Wilner, Danny Randell, Logan Miller, Aaron Shepard, Andrew Bodnar, Jason Russo, Peter Koutros, Robert DeVita, William Storz, Mike O'Brien, Bobby Denver, Dan O'Shea, Michael Manna, Jared Bell, Trevor Blenman and Anthony Spadaro -- all provided assistance and support throughout the book process as well.

And my fellow media members/colleagues -- Colin Stephenson, Steve Zipay, Matt Calamia, Arthur Staple, Nick Holmer, Amanda

Borges, Martin Biron, Josh Bogorad, Ryan Braithwaite, Brendan Burke, Butch Goring, Annie Fariello, Scott Charles, Ryan Chiu, Steve Valiquette, Charlie Cucchiara, Jeff Day, Bob de Poto, John Fayolle, Matt Fineman, Jim Fox, Jim Gallagher, Shannon Hogan, Eric Hornick, Leo Scaglione Jr., Rachel Krawsek, Glenn Petraitis, Joel Mandelbaum, Dan Marrazza, Jim Matheson, Matt McConnell, Patrick McCormack, Robert Taub, Bob Melnick, Emma Miller, Bobby Mills, Mollie Walker, Hayley Cohen, Samuel Sandler, Lucky Ngamwajasat, Brad Polk, Larry Roth, Sarah Servetnick, Leslie Treff, Ray Katz, Mike Schreck, Neil Malvone, Colleen Wagoner and Alyse Zwick -- all of whom (along with those who I interviewed) helped to influence and guide my career.

SOURCES

"1949-50 New York Rangers Roster and Statistics." *Hockey-Reference.com*, www.hockey-reference.com/teams/NYR/1950.html.

"1978-79 New York Rangers Roster and Statistics." *Hockey-Reference.com*, www.hockey-reference.com/teams/NYR/1979.html.

"1993-94 New York Rangers Roster and Statistics." *Hockey-Reference.com*, www.hockey-reference.com/teams/NYR/1994.html.

"2011-12 New York Rangers Roster and Statistics." *Hockey-Reference.com*, www.hockey-reference.com/teams/NYR/2012.html.

"2013-14 New York Rangers Roster and Statistics." *Hockey-Reference.com*, www.hockey-reference.com/teams/NYR/2014.html.

"New York Rangers Franchise Index." *Hockey-Reference.com*, www.hockey-reference.com/teams/NYR/index.html.

****NOTE: All interviews were conducted either in-person or over the phone in order to obtain the necessary quotes and information.*

ABOUT THE AUTHOR

Matthew Blittner, born and raised in Brooklyn, New York, has been covering the New York Rangers and New York Islanders for multiple publications since the beginning of the 2016-17 NHL season. Along the way, he has covered: the New York Rangers 2016-17 playoff run against Montreal and Ottawa; the Rangers Road to the 2018 NHL Winter Classic; the 2018 NHL Winter Classic; the retirement ceremonies for Jean Ratelle and Vic Hadfield; the introduction of David Quinn as the 35th Head Coach in Rangers' history; as well as nearly every Rangers game since the start of the 2017-18 season.

Among the publications Matthew Blittner has written for are: MSGNetworks.com, The Fischler Report and NY Sports Day.

In addition to his responsibilities covering the NY hockey scene, Matthew obtained his Master's Degree in Sports Management from CUNY Brooklyn College in February of 2017 -- graduating with Summa Cum Laude honors.

Matthew's new book, Unforgettable Rangers, details the most significant games and moments in the careers of the broadcasters and writers who have covered the team, for generations.

Visit his Facebook page at https://www.facebook.com/UNFORGETTABLERANGERS/ or on Twitter @MatthewBlittner.

Made in the USA
Middletown, DE
19 January 2019